DREAMER

MICHAEL K JOHNSEN

BookBaby

//|BookBaby

DREAMER
Published by BookBaby

First published by BookBaby 2021
www.bookbaby.com

Cover Design by Julie Overberg | www.julieoverberg.com
Cover photo by Nick Fewings on Unsplash
Type setting by Julie Overberg | www.julieoverberg.com
Back cover photo by PURE FOTOGRAFICA | www.purefotografica.com
Printer BookBaby

Ordering Information:
For details, contact: michaelkjohnsen@gmail.com

Print ISBN: 978-1667801308

Printed in the United States of America on SFI Certified paper.

First Edition

I wrote this book for my kids and my family who believed in me. I couldn't have done any of this without a little voice in my head telling me to just keep going, not to listen to anybody, and do what I set out to do. Win!

CHAPTER 1.

It shouldn't have happened the way it did. I should have been a disaster from the start, a lost cause, maybe in jail. I would never have guessed how much I would eventually accomplish in such a short period of time, or that I'd end up in a position of power despite everything.

I was never the smartest kid, so I knew my gift of gab was going to be what propelled me forward in life. I was a child of humor from birth, and this laughter was my source of joy in life. As much as I was proud to have the ability to bring a positive light and joy to those around me, I didn't always have the maturity to control my self-expression, and at times, that got me into trouble.

My earliest memory of my big mouth getting me into trouble was the day I cursed out a nun at my Catholic school in the fourth grade. That day was pizza day, one of the best days at school and something I looked forward to. I wasn't the best student, and my homework was often a mess. At a young age, I already had a chip on my shoulder since my dad wasn't around, and the nuns had me pegged as a troublemaker from day one. On this particular pizza day, when it was time to turn in assignments, I was the last one to raise my hand.

The nun raced over to my desk like a tent in a hurricane and told the rest of the class they could make their way to the cafeteria. I was already feeling sorry for myself when her hand snaked out, physically striking me. She was probably about as shocked as me in that moment, but I wasn't silent for long. I let fly with all the worst curses my 9-year-old brain could remember. I apparently had a good memory for such things. It drove her crazy, a fourth-grade child telling her where to get off.

Although I got in trouble with the school, that's nothing compared to the trouble the school got into when my mother found out. She stormed into the school like a cat out of hell, ripping a new one into the nun, the other school staff, and anyone else who dared to get in her way. It would be right to say, our relationship with Catholic education came to an end, and from that day forward, I attended public schools.

My mother was well known in town, and not just for her ability to bring the wrath of God down on anyone who dared lay hands on her admittedly obnoxious child. She'd had me when she was 18, but that hadn't stopped her from making a career for herself. She had been building up her business and local reputation in our small town in Florida through her brilliance in marketing. By the time I was ten, I couldn't say my last name in town without everyone knowing who my mother was. That day in fourth grade was the first time I saw my mother really have my back. At first I was afraid to tell her about the situation, thinking she was going to be on the nun's side. Instead, all she could say was, "How dare that old bitch hit my baby!" I'll never forget that; it was the first time I felt such a strong sense of security and confidence.

I really needed some sense of security, because in many ways, I didn't always feel like I was on solid ground. My mother had tried her best to give me everything a child should have, but there was no way she could make up for my absent dad, who I didn't meet until I was around ten years old. I did have a stepfather, but I didn't have a lot of respect for him. His son, my stepbrother, was a few years older than me and one of my best friends. We made tree forts and worked together to break every rule possible when we weren't doing skits for my parents or seeing who the best one was at Nintendo.

Our family lived in a traditional all-American neighborhood in the suburban back roads of our medium-sized Southern town. We had nothing too fancy, but we felt safe and comfortable in our three-bedroom house with the swing set in the backyard alongside a slightly rickety above-ground pool. We enjoyed Easter eggs hidden every spring and Christmas lights every December.

I was still pretty young when my stepfather and mother had my younger brother, and that's when the competition in life really began. My brothers and I were always competing for everything, especially our parents' attention.

Back then, in the early nineties, life was a lot different. Most of the time, the best source of entertainment we had was each other. My brothers and I competed constantly and fiercely. Whether it was sports, video games or just seeing who could climb the highest tree, it was always a race to be number one. We competed to see who could make the best fort in the trees behind the house, or raced handmade paper boats in the bathtub. Everything between me and my brothers was a contest. As I got older, I realized that this constant competition helped me develop a fiercely competitive attitude. While my brothers and I were just running around the neighborhood playing cops-and-robbers, I was learning true grit.

We didn't only compete; we also had a lot in common and had a great time together sharing music and hobbies and commiserating on how to deal with the parents. The first concert we went to was MC Hammer, and yes, we were all three rocking the hammer-time baggy pants. My mother loved Top 40 radio in that era. Instead of bedtime stories, I was put to sleep with Bananarama and Culture Club. That playlist stuck with me through my life.

My stepfather and I always had our differences. From a young age, I was rebellious from not having a father, and he was doing his best trying to replace that piece of my life. He didn't mistreat me when I was young, but I couldn't help but notice that he treated me differently than my brothers. I felt the lack of attention and nurturing that he naturally gave to his "real" sons. I was keenly aware of what they had that I didn't: the experience of a loving father tucking me in at night, saying "I love you. I'm proud of you." Of course, this disparity just made me want to impress him more, and I knew comedy was the one thing I had to offer. Although it never made up for the part I felt was missing from my life, I knew I could make him laugh and smile when I wanted, which brought me some comfort and reassurance that I would be valued by the man of my household. He especially got a kick out of it when my brothers and I made homemade commercials on our videorecorder and acted out silly parts from stupid infomercials on TV. Iit was one of the times we had a real connection and bond.

Although there was natural friction in the house, for the most part everything was pretty great until my brothers and I hit the middle school years. My brothers were still in Catholic school while I was fighting the inner-city kids in dodgeball and city league sports at my public school. I was having hard times, both socially and with my grades. I had low self-esteem, and I spent a lot of time looking to get attention anywhere I could. I often felt that I was the only one on my side, and I had to be the one to lift my own spirits or reassure myself that I could be good at anything. It was hard to fit in and find my place, so naturally I started to rebel.

Instead of paying any attention to lessons, I would spend all my time entertaining my classmates, being the proverbial "class clown." For example, If I wasn't making fun of my teachers and doing impressions of the principal, I would be pushing a grocery cart around the classroom, reenacting Supermarket Sweep, while my poor teachers struggled to get control over me. We had a lot of fun, but my behavior was really a result of my growing insecurity from my lack of paternal attention. My grades couldn't have been any lower, and despite getting laughs, I felt more and more down on myself. The only reason I made any effort at all in my academics was in order to stay qualified to play sports.

Sports became one of the only things that were important to me. Playing baseball and hockey at a young age showed me and others that I was good at something, and I started getting people's attention. It was a big boost of accomplishment when I made a big hit that won a game or stopped a puck in a crucial moment at the end of a hockey game. When I failed to make good grades, I grew even more critical of myself in a self-reinforcing downward spiral. Meanwhile, the atmosphere in my family life at home had degraded into a state of constant tension, my stepfather becoming more violent as I got older. I really needed the distraction of laughter before I left school each day. I had nothing to look forward to at home.

Getting down on myself was an ongoing problem for me. I knew my lack of confidence and self-worth was getting in the way of me achieving my goals, but I had no idea how to master my self-regard. Self-confidence was something I was always trying to understand and teach myself, and humor and sports were the only things that seemed to help.

CHAPTER 2.

When my struggles became overwhelming, I found ways to escape. For example, during my early high school years in the early 2000's, I watched the movie *Rudy* over and over until anyone else probably would have been sick of it. I began practicing kicking field goals in my front lawn every day, imagining three seconds left on the clock to defeat my rival and having it all come down to the last-second kick. Escaping into my imagination became a big part of my life.

Another important sport in my life was roller hockey. I was a big hockey guy, and I would skate all day and sometimes all night. Playing football and being in roller hockey leagues throughout my childhood really helped me to develop a stronger sense of myself, as well as gain valuable peer relationships through teamwork. Team sports truly gave me the confidence to overcome my self-doubt, and to stop letting small things affect me in my everyday life. I had always lived for competition and wasn't afraid of much in life. I always thought I could do anything if I worked my hardest and gave everything I had.

In my freshman year of high-school, I found myself on completely unstable ground. I went from the football field to detention pretty fast. If I wasn't dodging punches from my stepfather, I was sneaking off campus for a cigarette, not really worrying about the next "F" grade I was always about to receive.

It all came to a head when I decided it would be fun to break into an old mental hospital, pretending I was in Ghost Adventures and investigating the paranormal. This hospital was huge, I mean eight stories and took up about two or three blocks. More importantly, it was completely off limits to kids like me. I convinced a couple of buddies to come with me, and when we broke into the back of the hospital through a small broken door, my heart was racing a million miles a minute. I had heard about people sneaking into this place but never thought I would have the balls to do it. This place was intense: electroshock therapy rooms, padded walls, old broken wheelchairs in the hallways, everything you would see in the movies including broken windows and blood stains on the walls.

After about an hour in this horror show, we started to see red and blue lights outside flickering through the windows. The ghosts became a secondary concern when the back door was suddenly kicked in and I found myself on the floor with a police officer telling me not to move and to put my hands in the air. I was arrested and stuck in the back of a police cruiser with both of my buddies. All we could do was watch all these officers on the radio and phones calling our parents and writing up reports. Fortunately, one of the guys with me was the son of a very prominent judge in town, and when that was revealed, the handcuffs came off quick. But then my mother pulled up. She was pissed off. After quite the conversation on our way home, my mother apparently decided she had had enough of me, and for the first time ever, she sent me off to my father. We never did find that ghost.

I can still remember the look of disappointment on my mom's face while she drove the eight hours to meet my father. It was the first time that I felt that I was truly on my own. At that point, I had developed a huge chip on my shoulder, and I had everything to prove. I thought playing football at my new school would be my way out again, but it just fueled the fire of my anger and resentment even more.

The first time my father ever saw me play football was in my early teens, 5 years after I had begun playing. I wasn't really expecting him to show up, so when I noticed him at one of our practices, I immediately felt the need to show off. During one of our drills in practice, all fired up on adrenaline, I tackled an unsuspecting kid and threw him over one of the training tables on the sideline. I got yelled at by the coach, and he told me that I was a troublemaker and there was no room for that on his team. Of course, I was still in full rebellious mode, so I smirked and ran laps for the rest of the practice. Really, I was trying to show my father nobody was going to push me around. My father, apparently, had other plans for me.

After getting in trouble on the football field and then skipping school afterwards, my father showed me exactly why my mother had kept me away from him and his bad temper. He beat me till I couldn't move, and worse, made it somehow seem like his behavior was my fault. I didn't fully understand how severe that beating was till the next day when I couldn't get out of bed.

By the time I dragged myself out of bed, my father had left for work, and right away I started calling my mom back home, saying something happened to me, and my back hurt bad. My mother told me she would come get me, but it was a long trip, so I had to take care of myself until then. I packed all my stuff (which wasn't much) and started thinking how to keep myself safe. Suddenly, the home phone rang. I picked up and heard my father's voice asking who I had been talking to. I became frightened. How did he know I was on the other line talking with someone? I had never been so afraid of what would happen next.

He told me he was on his way home and hung up the phone fast. I had to think quickly, so I put all my bags and personal stuff in the corner and waited for him to pull in the driveway. It felt like hours, but it was likely only about twenty minutes before I heard his car pull in. I ran to his room where I knew his army knife was, and then locked myself in the bathroom. I heard the door open, then my name being called. I ran from the bathroom and found myself in between my father and the front door of the house. I had the knife in one hand, and my heart was beating out of my chest. I didn't know what he would do, but I said, as fiercely as I could manage, "If you touch me again, I'm going to defend myself."

I wasn't ready for his response. When he looked at the knife, he just said, "What are you going to do with that?" in a mocking tone. The fight-or-flight reactions that I had been homing in sports suddenly kicked in--I opened the door and ran. I had no idea where I was going. I just took off like I did on the football field. I knew there was a gas station close by, so I ditched the knife in the woods and kept running.

When I finally showed up at the gas station in terror over what had just happened, an employee called the police. My last experience with the police hadn't been fun, but it was nothing like the embarrassment I felt when I had to take off my clothes in front of this cop and show him the bruises and cuts on my back. They took me back home in the police car. My father was outside waiting and didn't look happy. The last time I saw my father, he was getting in the back of a police car with handcuffs on, smiling at me the whole time, saying "Thanks a lot," and, "Look at what you have done." I had never been more confused and alone than in that moment, but somehow, I knew this situation wasn't really my fault, and before long I was returned to my mother.

Things were different when I returned: my mother and my stepfather were not getting along at all, and at the same time, her business was on the rise. By the time I was finishing my freshman year, I had started to turn into a party boy, sneaking into clubs and watching DJs. It quickly turned into a habit. At age fifteen, I had already learned a level of self-reliance between being out till two in the morning and covering my ass by inventing stories on where I had been when I finally made it home. My stepfather and I fought as much as we always had, but soon he and my mother were even worse. I was pretty sure they were heading towards divorce, and finally one day, my mother had had enough. Her business was growing rapidly, and his insecurities couldn't take that; he was very old-school, and his wife making more money and being in the spotlight wasn't something he could handle. So, she and I moved.

CHAPTER 3.

Now it was just my mother and I and occasionally my younger brother, per custody agreement. I was off to a new high school. Of course, I still had the same need to prove myself, and that came out on the football field, but with my stepfather out of the way, my home life stabilized, and I was finally feeling like a normal kid.

I became even more involved in partying, both planning and attending, but one of the most significant events of that year was the time I met a DJ and went to a huge college club on a school night. I met the guy at a live broadcast the radio station was doing, and when he was done talking, he told me I should come with him after. I think he thought I was older than what I really was, but I went with the flow and met him in front of a bar. I wasn't dumb; I should have been eighteen to enter and twenty-one to drink, but that didn't stop me. When he walked in, I walked right behind him like I worked for the radio station, and nobody stopped me. I drank and partied till 2am and knew I had to find a way home and be in class first thing in the morning. Showing up to school hungover and still wearing the same clothes just showed that I was willing and ready for anything.

Sophomore year came, and we were kings of the school. There were only freshmen and sophomores at the high school I attended after the divorce, so my buddies and I were like the seniors that year going in. At that time, I was one of the more popular kids, mainly focused on trying to make a mark on the football field. The only thing I really had to worry about was staying out of trouble and doing well with grades and sports.

With my newfound freedom and a calmer home life, I was able to discover new ways to channel my energy. Music had always been a big motivator in my life and, in the late nineties, everyone wanted to be a DJ. So did I.

I remember the day I received my first set of turntables. My mother got me my first set of Numark belt-drive turntables. In my mind, this was a release from everything. They almost felt like my way out, the thing to make me disappear in my own little world. After receiving my new instrument in life, the next thing I did was start borrowing old house vinyl's to spin. At one point I was even in a local band as a scratch DJ, and I couldn't help but imagine I was playing in the next Slipknot concert. Things were going great. I didn't have a real plan for the future, but I was enjoying being a kid.

Football was everything to me. Not only had I played for two different high schools by now, but here I was the oldest and biggest on the team. My mother was, as always, my biggest fan, and she even traveled to watch me play.

However, my attitude outweighed my talent, and I more often found myself in trouble than in games. Once after an unsportsmanlike penalty in a big game had sent me to the bench, I was starting to see red. This was a big game and the first of the season. I was sitting there feeling frustrated as the game wrapped up when some woman came over and told me I needed to be in the team huddle and to get off the bench. In that moment and not knowing who this person was, I told her that it wasn't my fault the team sucked, and she could kiss my ass.

The woman was the coach's wife. I soon found myself doing

sprints while everyone else got to take showers and change clothes.

There was a coach on the team who had it out for me. I'm sure I didn't go out of my way to change his opinion of me, but this guy was a dick, and he was looking to take it out on someone. After one practice, he informed me that he didn't like my attitude and made me run 100yd dashes, hitting the ground after every whistle. After about thirty minutes or so, I had had enough. I told him to get his pussy ass out there and let me blow the whistle! He swore and began marching toward me, obviously ready to rip into me. Never one to stand down, I launched myself toward him. I swear, I had "Let's get ready to rumble" playing in my head as we both charged each other on the football field. Other coaches broke up the fight, but the head coach pulled me aside and had a conversation with me inside the locker room. He told me I was a good football player, but I needed to work on my attitude before next season. I also learned that he had decided not to play me in the final two games, but I could return for winter workouts. This was a big blow to me, but his decision made sense, especially after what had just happened between the other coach and me. I had friends on the team, including my best friend, who was the quarterback, and it was hard to not be playing football with them. But nothing was going to prepare me for what happened next.

It started like any other day. I woke up, drove to school, and pushed through the front doors as usual. Once inside, however, I got the cold shoulder from everyone in the hallways. Even teachers were looking at me weird. A buddy came up to me and said, "Nice job. You really did it this time." I had no clue what I had done! As I was wondering why everyone was so upset, someone pulled out the front page of the local newspaper, and it had an article about me. The headline read: "HIGH-SCHOOL FORFEITS ALL GAMES DUE TO INELIGIBLE PLAYER."

I was confused and in shock as I tried to skim the article for more information. All football players had to keep up minimum grades to stay on the team, so I'd been careful to skirt that line. The paper informed me that some player had managed to get onto the team despite bad grades, and he had played in one of the bigger games. When the board found out that he was ineligible, our school was forced to forfeit all of the regular season games. My stomach twisted and my head was spinning. I slouched into my first period class, which was taught by the coach I had just fought. He opened up the day by explaining what was going on.

"A horrible thing has happened to our football team. The student responsible for it should feel ashamed of what he did."

Holy shit, I thought, looking around the classroom at the shocked and angry faces of all of my classmates, *he's talking about me.*

"Because of his actions, this student will no longer be allowed to play sports again at this school. No other school is likely to accept him into their sports programs either, so his football career is as good as done. In fact, with his bad grades, I'm surprised he hasn't just dropped out already."

He went on and on, but I'd had enough. After hearing this guy badmouth me and explain how bad of a person I was, I left his class and went to my car to read the entire newspaper article. In it, I learned that apparently, I had been ineligible to play all along because of the grades that had transferred from my last school. When the coaches and staff found out, they immediately kicked me off the team, but they still had to give up their season.

I crumpled the paper. This was all lies, and I was furious. I had nothing to do with my own grades transfer, and if they messed up, that was on them. I had played the whole year without hearing anything about grades or eligibility. They clearly kicked me off the team because of a fight, and not because of grades, and I was not invited back for the next season. I basically felt like the football staff wanted to cover their asses because they were all new hires, so they were throwing me under the bus for the forfeit. I was pretty sure that was the worst day of my life, and I was only sixteen.

I had barely gotten to my next class when I was sent to the principal's office and given two options: leave school or spend half of my school days in a disciplinary school. I said no to both options, speaking my mind how this was completely unfair and not right.

So, they said goodbye, and I dropped out the next day.

Depression is a funny thing. I thought I was headed straight back to my self-deprecating thought spirals, but I had to work. I had no GED, no resume, and no trade. When my mother found out what had happened, she was on my ass to find a job immediately. Don't get me wrong, at this point she was very well off, and I could have sat on my ass and lived off her paychecks. But that's not the way I was raised, and I knew there was something else out there for me. I just didn't know what.

Luckily, I had made some friends who were always there for me with strong emotional support. One friend helped me set me up a construction job. It wasn't a bad job by any means, and shit, I was making more than any of my friends and most adults. I was still sixteen, though, and it was very hard waking up at five AM six days a week to go to work and then coming home ten hours later to crash and do it all again the next day. I saw my life turning into being a working man with no education, living in the same town I was from and trying to accept it. This was not for me, and I knew I had to change something fast and by any means possible.

CHAPTER 4.

Three months after turning seventeen, I woke up and decided enough was enough. I called in sick and sat around my mother's house, thinking about what my next move in life would be. It was a difficult decision because this was a good job, I was planning on leaving.

All day, I thought a lot about what I really wanted out of life and how to get there. I knew I loved entertaining people, but I really wasn't sure what direction to take that idea into. In my head, I was the funniest and most entertaining person I knew. In reality, I was just a wannabe club DJ like a lot of other guys with big dreams and no clue.

I called a friend to talk over some ideas, and he suggested I call one of his ex-girlfriends. She worked at the local radio station and would know if they were hiring. He had known me for a few years from being in the club scene and was a well-known DJ at that time, so I said *what the hell* and tried to get in touch with this ex-girlfriend. That one phone call changed my life.

It turned out that this girl was the biggest afternoon drive personality in my town. Everyone knew her voice. Just to get a chance to talk to her, I called up the request line. That afternoon, she happened to be holding some kind of impression contest on the air, and she was live on the biggest drive-time listenership of the day. So, I dialed in.

When she picked up the request line, I told her who I was, and how my friend had dated her back in the day. She laughed and then asked me if I could do a Chewbacca impression. Since all the other ones had sucked, she said she really needed a winner. It was like a dream-come-true scenario for me. It was the middle of the afternoon, and instead of being at work, I was standing in my living room in my underwear doing my best to sound like Wookie, and most importantly, making this DJ laugh out loud. She agreed to have me come down to the radio station to meet her and take a tour.

Showing up at one of the biggest Top 40 radio stations in the city was exciting but nerve-wracking. I knew for sure that she liked my personality on the phone, but what kind of impression would I make on her when we met in person?

I drove down to the station, palms sweating, trying not to think anything negative. I walked in the door with as much confidence as I could. She greeted me warmly and introduced me to her intern. We walked around a bit, and then she asked, "I'm doing a live broadcast at the club tonight. You wanna come?"

"I'm only seventeen," I replied, "but I have the best fake ID in the world."

She laughed and said, "Come on out." I don't think I could have driven any faster out of that parking lot, excited and motivated to do anything I could to impress her enough to give me a chance.

In 2001, the rave and techno scene was the place to party, and I was the poster child for this genre. That evening I spent at least two hours to create my look. I dug through my closet rejecting shirts to go with my black pants. I mussed my hair correctly and topped it off with a silver hoop earring. I was guaranteed to make an impression.

I showed up an hour earlier than the DJ and made sure that

I was ready to do anything I could to make her night easier from the moment she pulled up in the big red radio station van. It was going to be a challenge to figure out what she needed, however. It was the first time I got to see exactly what a normal DJ would do to set up a live broadcast.

When she arrived, I was right there asking what I could help bring into the club. This brought a smile to her face, and we started to walk in through the crowd of people waiting outside. At that point I felt like a rock star; she had everyone waving and saying hi. Inside, all the bartenders were waiting with open tabs and a private room for her to use. She got right to work. First, we had to set up a table and banner and a display for the giveaways she was doing. Then she got her recording equipment set up and found a cell phone signal so the board operator back at the station could record her 60 second spots. It wasn't much, but I was sure that I could convince the DJs that they really should have a radio intern to help their every need. Once I'd helped her set things up, I just had to wait and see if she needed anything else. I wasn't there to act like I was the celebrity. I didn't know shit, and I was so humbled by everything going on. I think she saw my dedication.

Before the club opened, I went outside and helped her sign up listeners for a giveaway she was doing. Then I broke down all the equipment to load in the van so she could relax. She started doing her live broadcast on the radio, and after hearing people in the background cheer and make it sound like the biggest party of all time, I was hooked and wanted to be a part of this lifestyle. Throughout the night, she would make announcements on the microphone and people would scream. The energy she brought was addicting and being next to her was inspiring. I was sure I wanted to be a DJ, and this was my way in. After that night, she wanted me back at the radio station to meet the program director (PD for short) and other DJs. I was amazed they wanted me back, not as a listener, but now maybe as an intern.

My confidence was turned down a notch when I walked into the actual radio station and saw the control board for the first time. It was the most intimidating piece of equipment I had ever seen. This thing looked like it should have been on a space shuttle with hundreds of buttons and microphones surrounding it. I started sweating and thinking, *I can never do this.* I might have been funny, and I could make people laugh, but I was sure I would never be handling something like that by myself.

When the DJ came into the booth, she was all smiles, obviously pleased that I had showed up and on time. I learned quickly that there was no point in being in radio if I couldn't be on time; the clock wouldn't stop because I couldn't wake up and make a shift. The first time doing a live show with her was a high. Answering phone calls and taking song requests could get aggravating for most DJs, but for me on my first day there, I couldn't have been more excited.

I was starting to get comfortable with the routine and demands of an actual show when she asked me a very important question, "Would you like to intern here and work on my show?" Like the fat girl finally getting asked to prom after waiting for weeks, I jumped into her arms and screamed yes. She said I would be helping at live events and working with her live on-air to run her show. It was awesome. She already had one intern, but I was determined to make the most of this opportunity and hopefully fall into a job I could only have dreamed of.

Walking into a radio station on the bottom level was like being the runt of the litter. Not only was I fearful of being fired at any time, I had to focus on watching and listening to every little thing so I could act like I knew what I was doing. The radio station was just like any small market broadcasting group: there were three stations, country, classic rock and Top 40.

I was the new kid on the block and getting to know everybody and making my personality known was a strong point of mine. It was my only choice because I had nothing but my sense of humor. The real big shot at the station was the program director, second only to the operation manager, at least on the programming side. This was the person I wanted to impress, and I tried everything I could to get his attention. If there was anything I could give, it was time, so I asked for everything and anything when it came to part-time board operating shifts or remote set ups.

The most public thing I did were the live remotes. Being on site, I'd not only be talking to listeners at events, but other radio groupies could get to know me as well. One day the DJ for the rock station asked me if I wanted to go with him to a live broadcast, he was doing for a couple bands at a small concert. I said sure, so we jumped into the radio station van and headed to the venue where the concert was happening. As we got out of the van, we were greeted with smiles and high fives, but to be honest, it wasn't that many people. I thought this was some big concert, but there were only a couple hundred people there. The rock DJ mentioned that the big attraction was a new band that had just started getting popular enough to get a song on the radio. After interviewing the band with him and hanging out backstage in their green room, I was trying to figure out who these guys were. When I learned that the band name was Disturbed, I didn't think much about it. I didn't know it then, of course, but within a few weeks they would blow up on radio and become one of the biggest rock bands of all time.

CHAPTER 5.

Around this time, the internet was starting to become a household thing. I know it's hard to imagine life without an iPad or smartphone now, but outside of cable TV, the entertainment those days was the radio DJs. Although music was always a draw, the DJ's personality was just as important. I had no idea how to do any of that. The best contribution I could make was making sure the T-shirts were folded and aligned perfectly. But I was learning, and every opportunity I could get watching these DJs do their routines either on the air or off the air was a free education for me.

My first time speaking on-air was nerve-wracking. I had made just enough of an impression for an afternoon show host to give me a shot on a certain topic she was discussing. The radio host took the first caller and let me talk to this listener. I was making fun of, let's say, a certain body part she had, and I was making not only the caller laugh, but the radio host as well. My first thought was, *Awesome; I did great,* but then a red flash of light started going off.

A phone I had never seen before started to ring. This was my first lesson in getting "red lined" and my program director had just heard it happen over the air. He was not happy. As soon as I picked up the phone, my ear began bleeding to the tune of, "Why did you say that? It wasn't funny."

"Of course, it was. Everyone laughed but you." The PD was

still not happy. I was recording the whole phone call and begged the afternoon show host to play it on the air. I mean, how good would that sound? The idiot radio DJ making fun of the ditzy blonde and then getting yelled at by the boss--comedy gold. She ended up playing it, which resulted in a flood of callers. It turned into a very funny radio bit, and I began to have some hope that I might have what it took to be on-air.

My five minutes of glory didn't stop me from doing my best as an intern. I spent every second and minute I had at the radio station. I did everything from cleaning out all the station vehicles to watching production directors cut tape and produce commercials. I felt like the more I knew, the harder it would be for them to get rid of me. Despite my best efforts, it looked like my days as an intern were numbered.

"It's time for one of your interns to go! I know the one is your best friend, so get rid of the other. I can't keep paying them both." I could hear the operations manager yelling from his office at the DJ host. It was right before the afternoon show started, and I knew I wasn't the DJ's best friend by any stretch of the imagination.

When she called me into the radio booth, I thanked her for the opportunity and let her know, "No hard feelings. It's business."

She looked at me and smiled. "You're not going anywhere." I was in disbelief. How could she keep me and let her best friend go? She told me I had talent, and one day with hard work I would become a solid DJ. This was a big boost to me. I had finally reached what I wanted to accomplish.

Up to that point, I was lucky to even get a part-time shift on the air, but the afternoon show was getting bigger every day. Not only did I have my mother on the air, embarrassing me every second, but after a while, even teachers that I'd had in the past were calling the show wanting to talk to me. I had to make myself known to the big bosses to get them to give me my own on-air shift. I decided to shoot for the night DJ position.

The night jock at a radio station was almost more important than morning or afternoon guys. This was the ultimate in entertainment. The night jock needed to have a crazy, outlandish, and cocky personality, so that was the image I aimed to create, and it shaped and formed my personality.

I spent as much time as possible with the guy who was running the night show. He was the number one-night jock in town, and everyone listened to him. The in thing in 2001 was a mix between cool and confident with a quick and fast delivery and watching him in his element was like watching a mad scientist in his laboratory. In between songs, he would have callers lined up on hold while coming up with his next song and winner call. When I came in, he had just enough time to tell me to sit before he started his next break. This guy was doing fifteen things at once and counting in his head how many seconds before the next break.

The night show was almost like a chess match: there had to be a strategy to ensure everything was working and it all sounded amazing. In radio, everything happens right down to the second, and a DJ has no time for mistakes or dead air. This guy did this every night, and not only that, but he would also play four phone calls and be talking six times per hour while handling a topic or giveaway at the same time. But it was worth it. This guy had every girl in the town calling. It was the dream job, and I couldn't wait to get into it.

He told me at the beginning, "I'll help you in any way possible. All you must do is show me you care. The minute that you stop, that's when I stop." From that day on, I didn't leave his side. I spent every day at the radio station, and even if they didn't have money to pay me, I still showed up. He told me stories about how he had started in radio in Minneapolis and how he'd learned under some of the biggest DJs in the country. I really learned a lot from him, but it wasn't always easy.

I would do this guy's errands, set up all of his live broadcasts and do anything I could to get on his nice list. The hardest thing for me to do was to shut my mouth. Not only did I listen to him, but at the time I was listening to every aircheck by the top DJs in the country. I would stay up until 4 AM every night listening to different DJs and their delivery and learning what it took to be a good night jock. Sounding good is one thing but putting together a show was something completely different. I would spend hours in a production room learning how to cut tape and put together phone calls to make the listener and myself not only sound funny but polished at the same time.

Even though I was spending all my waking hours dedicated to radio or helping the night DJ, I was barely getting paid. One day the program director came up to me saying, "Sorry, we just don't have the money right now." The station had more than enough part-timers and full-timers, and they didn't have room for another hire.

"Honestly? I'm learning so much, if you keep me on even for an hour, I'll stay and do everything for free." Eventually even management started to notice my drive. I mean, come on -- who would not love the kid that shows up and stocks everything that they had for a live broadcast, cleans the radio station and co-hosts an afternoon show for free?

At that point in my life, I decided money was not going to stop me from becoming a good DJ. I wanted to be the best, and nothing was going to stop that. I worked two other part-time jobs just to keep this going. At night, if I wasn't at a club working for the radio station, I could almost always be found at the night jock's apartment listening to airchecks and learning how to do breaks. This guy hadn't just come from nowhere. Before moving to my state, he'd worked for one of the top radio stations in Minneapolis under one of the biggest DJs in the country.

Despite all my dedication to the radio station, I still had football aspirations in my head, so in between breaks, or when I was bored, I would go outside and kick field goals for hours in front of the radio station between two huge pine trees. This lead to some good-natured teasing, and some of the guys called me the "Rudy" of the radio station. At one point, I admit I missed a field goal and took out one of the radio antennas. I thought that would be my last day at the radio station, but the operations manager laughed, and said, "Well, we saw this coming."

Free labor and football weren't the only things I did as part of the radio station. The biggest club nights of the week were obviously Thursday, Friday and Saturday, and walking into a club with an all-access pass for the biggest radio station in town not only got me perks but also attention from everyone. Just pulling up in the radio station van brought stares from a line of clubbers looking to see who would jump out.

I met one girl at the hottest club of the time. She was a club groupie, but after going on a few dates with her, and finding out she was the President's niece, I started to feel like a big shot. Maybe my ego was getting the best of me. Being in clubs and in front of celebrities started to feel normal. Although I was only 17, it taught me a level of responsibility I never let go of. I couldn't just show up in a radio station van carrying radio station gear and act like an idiot. My program directors would always say, "You are always representing the radio station, and we will fire your ass if you show your ass." This was hard sometimes.

I would be out until early morning every night of the week

with the biggest DJs in town and then have to get back to the radio station on time to cover for somebody after a long night of partying. There were certainly some rough days, but my persistence made an impression on my bosses. I was working for nothing and would do everything. They could always rely on me, even when I had the worst hangovers in the world (which happened at least three times a week).

I began spending more time learning how to put a show together, spending countless hours listening to DJs around the country so I could implement their techniques for my own style. Being on a Top 40 station, I had to have the right sound, and my Southern country-ass accent was starting to become a problem. Don't get me wrong, I didn't fake one thing about my own personality at any point in this story, but if I wanted to sound solid and get a radio job outside of my small town, I had to have the right style.

My mentor suggested reading the newspaper and magazine articles out loud, which was a useful trick that really helped me over the course of a couple months. My persistence was paying off, and I was handling weekends and filling in shifts during the week. Any shift I could get, I would take, no questions asked. My goal was to show the bosses I was ready to handle a show by myself, and the more experience in it, the better.

I worked hard to not only become technically proficient but to build my style. One day, I had a friend in the radio booth with me who said, "Man, you have the easiest job in the world, all you have to do is talk to people on the radio and push buttons."

Haha! I spun one of the guest mics in front of him pressed the on-air button and said "Here, you do it then!" He froze, and that's when I proved to myself that I had what it takes to make it in the business, and it was up to me on how far I could go.

CHAPTER 6.

Everyone knows where they were on 9/11/2001. For me, I woke up to a phone call from my mother telling me to turn on the news, saying "the end of the world is happening." Watching planes hit the world trade center was like watching a movie. It didn't look real, and I remember thinking, *this is not really happening*. The first thing I did was jump in my car and head to the radio station. Remember, I was just doing weekend air shifts at that time and the occasional live broadcast. But I knew things would be crazy, and I wanted to help out in any way possible.

After sitting with other DJs watching the news unfold, we started getting faxes of Do Not Play List, a list of songs radio stations couldn't play because they involved the word "bomb" or referenced people dying. The situation was weird from the broadcasting side, and I spent a lot of time listening carefully to make sure I was following the correct procedures as we worked to inform our listeners what was going on.

I was waiting to go on the air with my mentor because I was still interning on the afternoon show, but she never showed up. I checked the clock. It was thirty minutes before the show was to start, and the host DJ was still missing. Radio doesn't stop because of tragedy, but she was also my best friend at the time, so I was doubly concerned. After waiting inside for her to show up, I went out to the parking lot and saw her sitting in her car with cell phone in her hands. She was crying hysterically. She was from Long Island, NY, and I realized her friends and family might have been in danger. Her parents worked in New York and commuted there every day, so of course in that madness she couldn't reach them. She refused to get out of her car and would not listen to me or even the operations manager who was outside talking to her. I went back into the radio station and called her boyfriend, who was a friend of mine, and told him to get there fast and come get her. As he pulled up, she started to calm down and got in his car to go home and figure out how to reach her parents.

In show business, there is a saying: "the show must go on," and this was about to be my first big test. The afternoon show was the #1 show in town, and at two o'clock, someone had to be in the booth when the on-air button was pushed. The operations manager turned to me and said, "You're going on in ten." My jaw dropped, and I wandered into the station again, my thoughts racing. I closed the door to the booth and got ready for two o'clock to hit.

You know those times when your palms are so sweaty that you leave damp fingerprints on paper? That was nothing compared to the case of nerves that hit me in that moment. I was looking at twelve different things at once and praying I wouldn't screw up too bad. The operations manager walked in and said, "Don't talk for more than 20 seconds. Just tell everyone we will update them on what's happening as it comes in."

For the first hour, it was a slow start and quick breaks with no upbeat personality. This was a learning experience for me because I was a playboy type shock jock, and now I had to be serious and deliver a solid broadcast. It was my responsibility to deliver this horrible news to people who might not have been aware of it. It was the first and hardest air shift of my career. I had always thought my first time would be putting callers on air and girls calling just to talk to me about funny topics. This was the opposite. I was addressing the public as a professional and getting an important message out on the air. I was able to relax as time went on, and I'm proud of how I handled myself that day. I also impressed my bosses more than I would have for being a cocky funny guy, and over the next few weeks, they began giving me more shifts on-air by myself during prime-time hours.

After a while, things started to come back to normal. I was filling in more during the daytime hours, and I was starting to make a reputation for myself. In Top 40 radio, I had to make myself different and edgy to turn someone's head or make someone think, *what will he say next?* This was something I thrived on. If there was one thing I could do well, it was to make women laugh. I didn't forget the men but worked to make them want to live my lifestyle on the air. This was a show, a theater of the mind, they call it. I was just being myself, talking about everyday life and situations that I thought were funny or comical dilemmas. I lived in the radio station after my first shift. I even brought a pillow and blanket just in case I was exhausted or working late on editing bits and different shows.

Around this time, I started working on demos and audition tapes of my best shows. I told the night jock, who was a big part of my upbringing in radio, that I aspired of having my own show.

"Are you prepared to move anywhere in the country at any given time for a full-time position in radio?"

I didn't hesitate. "Yes."

"The only way you're going to have your own show is to move out of this dinky town. And don't take no for an answer."

Believing in myself was something I had to work hard on. Some people are told 'No', and they fall apart. I always searched for a Yes and never took No for an answer. I was told that when I auditioned for radio positions, I'd have about five seconds to catch attention of the program director, otherwise the demo would be tossed in the trash. This happened to me every day. Coworkers and mentors showed me how to research radio stations that were hiring and how to track down the address or email for the program directors to get my demo in front of them.

One by one the rejections started. If I wasn't getting a rejection email, I would get nothing at all. On the air I sounded good, but on paper I was a nobody-- no education, no real major market experience, and seventeen years old. I sent out over five thousand emails all over the country and was told the same thing: no.

I decided to try a different approach. I began to always put a request for suggestions at the bottom of emails so different program directors could give me pointers or in case they knew somebody else who was hiring. I hit a dead end, but I didn't let that stop me. I just had to get creative. I hunted day and night, sending emails and even packages with flowers and chocolates to kiss their asses. Nothing worked.

Finally, I asked around the station if anyone had friends in the business so I could get my stuff in front of someone. This led to my first audition and trial run for one of those bigger jobs I was looking for. A DJ at another radio station in town had a friend in Memphis who was looking for all day parts. He needed a morning, afternoon, and night jock for a new radio station they were building. I jumped at the opportunity, but I knew before going that this was just practice. I was pretty sure they wouldn't hire me, but I wanted to have experience being interviewed. In my mind it was a must, in case if a big station called, so I was ready to go.

After I had sent my stuff and contacted the station, they invited me up to Tennessee, and I stayed overnight to audition for the morning show job at six AM. This was new to me. I had mostly been on afternoon shows and some weekend shifts, often with another DJ looking over my shoulder. Now I was faced with doing a full morning show on my own. I wanted these people to take me seriously so I could build up my courage to step into a major market and own the microphone.

Walking into the Memphis radio station and meeting the crew wasn't intimidating. Me acting like I knew what I was doing, made it nerve-racking. I mean, this was a midsize market with radio guys that had been in the business for years, and I was this cocky new Top 40 jock walking through the hallways with my chest out. I put on my confident persona, but this was all for show; I was scared shitless, desperately trying to hide the fact that I felt like I was going to puke.

I left all that at the door when I hit the microphone and came out with some basic liners from the liner book about where the station was going to broadcast live around town and sponsors for the hour. I thought this was what they wanted to hear, but the assistant program director came kicking in the door and said, "quit reading liners and fuckin' talk already."

OK, asshole, you want it, you got it. I switched to what I was good at and soon had a waiting list of calls from every woman in Memphis that wanted to be on the show. I put together live calls and funny topics and nailed the interview. Country guys get called out a lot for being lame, so I made it into a joke. I had women of Memphis being auditioned for a blind date with me. I told them to leave the boots on the porch and come out with a city boy for the night. This had them fired up. I would have women call up and say how country boys didn't do it for them and they wanted a city boy to show them the ropes. I played the part and had them giving me their sexy voices live on the air to impress me for a date.

This was a big step in the right direction, and I was offered a full-time position for the morning or night show, whichever one I wanted. I respectfully declined and kept on looking for the right station and town to take over. In all reality, I should have taken this job since nobody was getting back to me by email. I needed experience, and this job would have given me that, so it was stupid of me not to take it. But I didn't want to go to Memphis, so I went back to my home station and pounded the computer with more emails. After that interview, I felt that I could go into a station and interview properly and not embarrass myself. I was building confidence in myself and the determination that I could be a great DJ one day.

Back at my home station, I had the drive to hit the emails even harder. My desire was to get back on the air, and I was ready to do so at any cost. Every email and day wasted, my regret for not taking the Memphis job grew, and I channeled my frustration into sending out more emails and demos. I was sounding awesome on the air and doing more live broadcasts. Becoming a part of the station and starting to be a respected DJ was a huge boost for my self-confidence. I was even working part time in one of the clubs where I broadcasted. My eighteenth birthday was celebrated with a suitable amount of partying, and I continued to hone my personality and style while learning how to be fast.

It's one thing to talk for thirty seconds about a sponsor or ad; it's another to carry a six-hour live show while cutting audio and running a board flawlessly. This skill didn't appear overnight; I spent hours of my days watching and listening to be good at anything. I would sit on the morning show dozing off or hungover while the host berated me to the public just so I could learn how to be fast and keep a show entertaining. I would watch the all-star night jock from six pm to midnight and take notes on what he did to be fast. The only way to survive in that industry was to be quicker and cleverer than the next guy.

Although I was getting good, sometimes I couldn't help but feel like I was doing it all for nothing. My email was still empty, and no stations returned my calls. I kept to myself most of the time, dedicated to finding that dream job and getting out of that small town, but a guy can't spend all his time alone. I always kept in touch with close friends from my school. While I was on the air, all my friends were finishing senior year and listening to my show in the afternoon.

CHAPTER 7.

One weekend a friend of mine was telling me about a huge storm that was going to hit. He came over to my house with a crazy idea.

"Come on, bro, these are going to be the biggest waves of the year. We need to go surfing!" I couldn't resist the opportunity and made plans to leave that night so we could surf early in the morning and beat this storm. We got into the car and began driving under a dense layer of clouds, but we didn't get far. We hadn't even gotten to the city limits before we ran up against a police barrier and a sheriff turned us around and said the road was closed due to the weather.

We tuned in to the local weather report on the radio, and it was bad. I shrugged, and we began heading home. It had already begun to rain, but the closer we got home, the worse the storm got. Everything around us started to flood. Even with the wipers going full blast, we could barely see twenty feet of road ahead.

We were crawling towards my neighborhood, battling the water that ran from the street into these huge drainage ditches when we started to lose traction. As we went around a bend in the road, I glanced towards the ditch and saw a light flashing inside a car that was floating on top of the water. I slammed on the brakes and started to back up. Someone was still in the car. They were about to hit the drainage pipe, which ran the risk of flipping the vehicle or pulling it all the way under water.

I jumped out of my car into the water to see what was going on. I grabbed the door handle and peered through the window. A guy and a girl were panicking in chest-high water. My friend was standing by the road, and I swam back and yelled to him, "Call 911. These people are going to die." I grabbed the car jack from my trunk and raced back to the floating car.

"I'm breaking the back window so you guys can get out!" I warned them before smashing the jack into it. The boy pulled himself out, but the girl was too big to fit through the window. I reached in and pulled up the lock so I could try and wedge her out. The water pressure on the car door made it almost impossible to push it open, but between the two of us, we managed to wedge the door open far enough that she could squeeze out.

All three of us climbed out of the ditch as the car was swept away by the current. Everyone was thankful nobody was dead. In that moment, I realized the boy was an old friend of mine. We waited for the police and the guy's father to get there. Once they he had confirmed that everyone was unhurt, my friend tried to explain.

"Sorry about the new car, Dad. We got washed off the road, and the electric windows and door locks stopped working, so we couldn't get out. I don't know what I would have done without..." but his father interrupted.

"I'm just glad you're all alive!" then he turned to me, "Thank God you were driving by!"

I went back home that night breathing a little harder but proud that I had stepped in and helped these guys.

The next morning, I went into the radio station with a great story to tell on the air, but the local media had already beat me to it. There I was, on the front page of the paper with a headline LOCAL RADIO DJ COMES TO THE RESCUE. This was my first time being interviewed for the local paper, so yes, my ego was a little big that day. This was something I could truly be proud of: I'd helped my fellow man. One of my coworkers took a picture of me wearing angel wings and holding the newspaper for my listeners to see.

At this point I was starting to get noticed by random people, and not just for being my mother's son for a change. My listener base was getting bigger by the day. Then, I received a phone call from the last person I would have imagined: the principal of my old high school. They were doing a big competition at the school and wanted me to host the event and talk about it on my radio show. She was on the phone telling me how proud they would be to have a former student and radio DJ to come host this event.

I interrupted her, "You remember when you basically forced me to drop out because I didn't have the right image for your school?" There was silence on the other end of the phone for a second, so I told her, "I'll do it, but only because I still have friends there, and I want to show them that even if people knock you down, you can still become something." There was another pause.

"You know," she said slowly, "you're right. Things didn't go as good as they could have. But you should still be proud of your accomplishments, and we'd still love to have you back to host the competition."

I got a lot of satisfaction out of her apology but realized there was no sense in being upset forever. I accepted the job and had them make a check out to me directly. Walking back into that school was one of my proudest moments. A year ago this school had wanted nothing to do with me and had embarrassed me more than anyone could. But that day they invited me back and even paid me to show up because all the students said I'd be the best choice. I tucked the check into my wallet, but it took me a week to cash it because I just enjoyed looking at it so much.

Coming back from this experience, I was more motivated than ever to find that big break. In radio, the one thing everyone bragged about was big market experience. Of course, there are always local guys who have only been at one station for decades, but most have been in different markets and all over the country. I think the night jock at my home station had worked in three different states and for four different stations. The one station he always liked talking about was a Top 40 in Las Vegas where he had worked part time.

I picked his brain for about a month on everyone who worked there and everything he did while on the air in Las Vegas. At that station, not just anyone could walk through the door. I couldn't even apply because they only hired jocks from credible stations with mid-market or higher experience and references.

I knew it would be a dream job if I could get it. I had been to Las Vegas once with my mother when I was fifteen. I had good memories of sneaking into casinos wearing a suit and playing roulette for free drinks. It would have been the coolest to be on the air in the entertainment capital of the world. Of course, this was a pipe dream if anything. My resume and demo didn't even meet the minimum requirements. But I figured the worst that could happen is the programming director would say no, just like everyone else. I didn't have anything to lose, so I sent the program director an email. As expected, I got no response.

At this point, I was sold on Vegas; I focused all my attention and time on getting a response from that important person. For a month straight I sent him an email every day, occasionally sending flowers to try to butter him up and get his attention. Besides. I sometimes called his work line just to hear his voicemail. I'm sure he was tired of hearing my voice and seeing an email after an email. I learned persistence in trying to get his attention. I had never even done this for any girl in my life at that moment or for anything at all for that matter. I wanted him to hear me and give me a shot, and I had nothing to lose calling him every day.

One morning I opened my email and saw the subject line: "Vegas On Air Opportunity". Talk about tears and emotion. I couldn't hit read fast enough.

"I couldn't help but notice you're willing to do anything and everything to get my attention. I currently have an opening for a part time and fill in DJ. Can you be here in two weeks?"

My hand was shaking as I slid the mouse to the reply button and typed, "Yes. Thank you. I'll be there right away. Thanks." I couldn't thank him enough. I was so grateful for the opportunity. He might have been tired of hearing from me, but he was willing to take a chance based on my limited experience and pure determination, although he knew that I wasn't really qualified yet.

Everything happened quickly after that. I got an email with the address, and suddenly, I had to prepare to move 2,300 miles away to get started on my dream job. I might have been crying when I told my friends at the station and my mom. This was what I had been working for, busting my ass trying to fit in and making a name for myself, and now it was time to take a chance. I was going to Las Vegas.

Leaving my hometown for the first time to a state on the other side of the country was like moving to another planet. I had money saved up from working, and my mother told me she would help me with travel expenses and apartment rental until I had a clue what I was doing. I had never traveled so far with so little idea how to get there, and now I had fourteen days to find an apartment, rent a moving truck, and figure out how to make a good impression on my new PD. This was 2002, and we didn't have GPS on our phones. I had to rely on old fashioned maps and printed directions from MapQuest.

I spent the next two weeks packing up my room, looking for hand me down furniture and anything else I could take with me on this journey. The night DJ who had first gotten me started dreaming about Vegas gave me the phone number for the apartment he had lived in, which was close to the station. I agreed to a lease over the phone for a one-bedroom apartment and sent out the deposits so I could check that off the list.

I realized right away I didn't want to drive all the way there by myself, so I racked my brains trying to think of someone who could spend a week taking turns driving the moving truck with me and helping me get settled in. Luckily, my mentor's boyfriend George, who I had hung out with more than a few times, agreed to make the drive with me if I flew him back when we got there.

My mother was an emotional wreck. She didn't even help me pack my clothes or move any furniture into the moving truck. It had always been just her and I, and until now, I was really the only thing she had full-time in front of her. My little brother was back and forth between houses, and her job wasn't as demanding now that she was well-established. I asked her if she was sad I was leaving, a dumb question in retrospect.

"Look, no matter how hard it gets there, you know there's nothing for you here. So go out there and make your mark."

I was eighteen years old at that time, and I'm sure she was overwhelmed. The night before I left, she showed up with about ten plastic moving bins filled with cleaning products, kitchen supplies and some other things I would need but hadn't thought of, having never been responsible for a home before. I knew she was proud of me; I just had to take full advantage of this new journey.

When I had everything loaded and ready, I stopped by my mother's office and said goodbye. I gave her a big hug and told her I wanted to make her proud.

"I'm already proud of you," she said before letting me go. With that, I hopped into the truck with my friend, and we left my hometown.

CHAPTER 8.

I don't think it had hit me yet what I was doing, but nothing was going to stop me from achieving my goal. The United States had always looked large on a map, but I had never realized quite how huge it was until I tried to drive across it.

"I can't believe I'm doing this," I burst out when George and I had been driving for a little while.

"It's going to be different. You've never been responsible for all your own bills and stuff," George said.

"It can't be that hard, can it?" I asked.

"No, I'm sure you'll be fine. But being on the other side of the country... no one is going to come bail you out if you screw up. And it's not like you can just go cry to your mamma if things don't work out."

I knew it was going to be a big change, but I couldn't help being excited. We talked and joked, but the further from home we got, the lonelier I felt, even with George there next to me.

I would have preferred to drive straight through, but when we got to El Paso, it was time for a break. El Paso, Texas, is right on the border of Mexico, which was a new experience for me. We rolled into town and stopped at the first Mexican restaurant we could find. With bellies full of fried rice and beans, we were in no mood to hit the road, so we found a strip club. I was still only 18, but I had plenty of practice getting into places with my fake ID. This one was different. George and I went in, got a table, and ordered beer. To my surprise, they told us they didn't serve alcohol, but if we wanted to purchase some at the gas station, the club was happy to provide ice. As we were walking across the street, George leaned towards me.

"Well, this is interesting," he said.

"We're totally going to get mugged, aren't we?" I replied.

Despite my worries and doubts, everything went just fine, and we were on our way again the next morning. We were heading to Phoenix to meet with the only person I knew that lived west of Florida. This guy was the biggest DJ in Arizona, but he had been my coworker at the home station when I was getting started as an intern. He was a bigger than life personality and took us to every big club in the city. Even though we hadn't seen each other in years, and we hadn't really known each other then, he sure did act like we have been best buddies since middle school.

"My house is your house. Just holler if you need anything and give me a call when you get to Vegas." Being in the radio industry was interesting in that way; every town had a radio station, and with the right connections, I could have gone anywhere and met up with a friend or a friend of a friend. This guy was more than happy to let us crash at his place after a long day of driving and a long night of clubbing, and he was genuinely excited for me and my new opportunity.

The next morning George and I got on the road and headed into our home stretch. Driving in the dessert for the first time was an experience all in itself. It felt like landing on Mars. Nothing looked familiar: there were no trees, no beach, no nothing, just dry flat land. I pulled over the rental truck just so I could walk and feel the sand. Of course, it was just sand, but it was different from the sand I was used to on the beach.

After making our way through Arizona, we approached the

Nevada state line and saw that Hoover Dam and the state line were only twenty miles away. My stomach clenched and my nerves went haywire. In a few moments I would be arriving in my new home, Las Vegas.

Except, we ran into a bit of a problem. September 11th fucked everything up in America. Not only were people scared of another attack, but our rights and privileges were also affected. I'd seen a few pictures of Hoover Dam and had watched Chevy Chase in Vegas Vacation, but I didn't know much about it. I was shocked to see that the road to Nevada was blocked by machine-gun-toting members of the US Army. Hoover Dam was under careful watch in case of attacks, and when we got close to the state border, an officer informed me I could not drive my rental truck over the Dam for security reasons, so I had to go all the way around to California and enter Nevada from the west.

Unlike modern GPS, printed directions do not automatically recalculate the route when you run up against a military blockade. It would take years for technology to advance beyond customized ringtones, so naturally I was nervous about change of plans. With a bit of encouragement from George and a lot of looking at the map, we were able to get by.

I saw the Vegas strip as we came in from Interstate 15, and it was the most overwhelming feeling of my young life. It's hard to explain what I was thinking pulling into this City of Lights. Seeing the Stratosphere and landmarks like MGM Grand and Caesars Palace was both exciting and nerve-racking. I felt like throwing up and rejoicing at the same time. Now, all I had to do was find the radio station and check in with my new home.

George and I drove around for a while before spotting a CBS radio sign under a conveniently conspicuous radio tower, and we were able to park the moving truck in the front lot. This is the first moment it sank in what was happening. I was now a radio DJ in Las Vegas. I was standing in the parking lot of one of the biggest Top 40 stations in the country.

I stood there, feeling very much like an eighteen-year-old kid in flip flops and a Florida State t-shirt. I walked up to the door, and one of my new coworkers let me in. Walking through the hallways of CBS radio was surreal. I was surrounded by radio booths and autographed pictures of celebrities. Then I walked into the main booth and saw my microphone for the first time. The board they were using was massive, and I could see twenty phone lines all lit up and the DJ at the time getting ready for his next break. I wanted to break down and cry like a little bitch. What had I gotten myself into?

When I was a kid, I had laughed at the movie Private Parts with Howard Stern because of how much he messed up and how bad he was on-air. Standing there in my new both, I could understand what Howard Stern had been going through. I freaked out. I wanted to get to escape and go back home. This was a mistake, and I couldn't bring myself to look for the PD or discuss signing my contract.

The DJ on-air pointed me toward an envelope with my name on it that my new boss had left on his door. I opened it to find a welcome letter, some food vouchers, instructions on how to check into my suite on the Strip and some other goodies as well. The station generously paid for a hotel for two weeks so I could set up my place in the meantime, but I was feeling so overwhelmed! I just wanted to find some place quiet to think.

I ran out of the radio station as fast as I could, got in my car and drove a hundred miles an hour to the hotel so I could contemplate what I was going to do. Panicking, I wanted to go home. I felt like this whole trip was all one big mistake and I made the stupidest decision of my whole life. What had I done?

How could I survive out here? How could I live in a place where I didn't know anyone and had no family or friends?

George sank into a comfy chair, enjoying the suite, while I was freaking out in the bathroom. Not knowing what else to do, I called my mom, hoping she could reassure me that giving up and coming home was a valid option. She had other ideas.

"Son, you've only been gone for three days, but today is the same as the day you left. I'm going to go home and have dinner at 6 just like I will every day until I die. You can't seriously think I'd be OK with you coming back to this. You're good at radio, and this is your big chance. People have been telling you all along that you couldn't do this, but this is your chance to prove them all wrong."

It took me a while to calm down and give this whole new life a chance. I kept telling myself not to give up and just keep trying to make the best of it. George was my saving grace. If it hadn't been for him, I don't know what would have happened. When I started turning into a nervous whiny bitch, he was there with a pep talk. George was a man that I respected, and his advice meant the world to me. He kept reassuring me this was a golden opportunity, and I couldn't throw it away. He walked me out to the balcony and showed me Las Vegas strip and said, "Look at this. Look at all of this. This is your time."

I looked at the Bellagio water fountains and the New York New York hotel and thought, *why not? What do I have to lose?* We headed out to walk the Strip, and by the time we were halfway down, I had started to come around and could at least breathe again. This city was fast, from the Casinos to the Clubs to all the hot girls walking around. I started to tell myself I could do this. CBS radio had chosen me to be on-air for the biggest pop radio station in Las Vegas, and from that point on, I started to believe in myself and my talent.

I took my time getting my apartment set up, and after a few days on the strip, I moved into my new home. Then, it was time to get to work, but first I had to drop off my friend at the airport for his flight back home.

As I pulled into the departure ramp, I was feeling nervous. George saw my clenched fingers, and before he got out of my car, he took his sunglasses off so he could look me in the eye and said, "You know nobody's coming home tonight, right?" This made me smile and want to punch him at the same time. He was right though, and I was finally ready to accept that. I watched him walk away with his carry-on bag, while I was driving off to go back to my new home.

CHAPTER 9.

I was worried my first night alone was going to be a repeat of my breakdown at the hotel, but thankfully it wasn't. Here I was, eighteen years old, two thousand miles away from anyone I knew, driving towards CBS radio to sign a contract to be an on-air personality in Las Vegas. I had no choice but to put on my big boy shorts and capitalize on this opportunity. I had been honing my cockiness and personality, but nothing prepared me for how I felt meeting the program director for one of the biggest stations in the country.

I could feel my palms sweating and a lump growing in the back of my throat. This guy was a legend, and he was in his prime. He didn't even shake my hand, just sat me down and started on what was expected out me from that moment on. He told me I was not allowed in any club or event that had to do with radio station where you had to be 21 to get in. The station could get fined or lose a license because I was underage. They were going to try me out in the overnight hours and weekends with limited shifts so I could get used to working the board and establishing myself on-air. I could tell that he was showing me he was the boss, and he wouldn't hesitate to send me home if I caused him any trouble. He also let me know that there was a lot of opportunity for those who played by the rules and performed well.

I sat nodding respectfully, making sure I didn't miss any fine print. Finally, it was time to pick up a pen and sign my name on the dotted line. And then it was done. I was officially a DJ at the biggest radio station in Vegas. Now remember, I didn't have a high school diploma, let alone a college degree, so I was hiding my big grin thinking, *Holy shit, what are the odds! There are guys who have been in this business for years and don't get this opportunity, and here I am.*

Once all the DJs found out there was a new kid on the block, I discovered that the rules were a little looser than the PD had led me to believe. I don't really remember the first night, but I got at least half a dozen invitations to clubs or strip joints with my new coworkers so they could show me the town. How could I say no, right? Typically, there are numerous lines outside the best night clubs, and if you're not on the VIP list, you very well may go home without getting a glimpse inside. Going to clubs with the DJs was not like that. They'd simply flash a CBS Las Vegas business card with their on-air name on the front, and the waters would part, and employees would be tripping over each other to give us the best service.

I had gotten used to being respected and even admired back at home, but this was like nothing I had ever seen. In Vegas, we would usually be escorted by private security through a side door to bypass both the line at the door and the big crowds inside. We'd be taken into a private VIP section or even straight to the DJ booth. The clubs were always hoping a DJ would pick up a microphone and start hyping everyone up on the dance floor. Chatting with celebrities and never paying for a drink were regular things. The first night I just watched everything amazed, but it was so easy to get into things, and I couldn't wait for my shot at the mic.

The biggest nightclub in Vegas in 2002 was RA at the Luxor,

and it was the first list I was put on. One night I had to get in by myself to meet one of the biggest DJs at the time. This was going to take some balls. Don't get me wrong; I'd had the best fake ID in the world since I was fifteen, so I was sure they'd let me in. I also had a business card with the station's logo on it, but no one really knew me yet. I put on a cocky grin and flashed my cards, and they let me right in with no questions asked. Walking into this club with celebrity-type status was one of the coolest moments of my life. I was told to show my business card to security after I got in so they would let me into the DJ booth.

I got to the end of the hall and couldn't help a rush of excitement. Beyond the stage, the DJs, and the mics, I could see thousands of people hyped up for a night of partying. I'd barely stepped out of the shadows when the DJs began talking me up. They high fived me and turned me toward the audience. I was blown away by the cheers and enthusiasm. I was on top of the world. The cocktail waitress came by, bringing bottles and mixers and never looked for anyone to take care of the bill.

I kept thinking my new boss was going to find out what was going on and fire my ass in two seconds. Not even a day after signing a contract, there I was on stage with a bottle of vodka in one hand and a microphone in the other, screaming at a crowd of people. But the DJs had my back.

"As long as you sound good, treat this in a responsible manner, and don't wreck yourself before your shift on the air tomorrow, nothing will happen, this is Vegas and this is your new job, own it."

One of my first tasks at the station was a concert we were hosting, and this was a major step in being around actual celebrities and taking on responsibilities. My new program director told me to be there to set up and get ready for this multi artist hip hop concert. Imagine P Diddy, Ja Rule, Little Bow Wow, Master P and B2K's first MTV concert. This was a big one, and as an on-air DJ, my job was to keep the energy up by talking between acts and getting the crowd hyped. There were about 30,0000 people in this crowd, and I was about to piss myself walking on stage. Only a month ago I had been patting myself on the back for hosting a club of a few hundred people, but now I was on one of the biggest stages set up in the country.

The day of the concert, I arrived ready to put on a show. I must have done well because the crowd was on its feet cheering. I remember walking off stage halfway through the lineup and seeing some girl trying to get my attention behind the wall of security.

"Hey, announcer guy! Can you give me that bottle?" she gestured frantically to Ja Rule's empty champagne bottle, which was lying on the ground near the stage. I ignored her and instead focused on psyching myself up for my next turn on stage. I flopped down in my chair and heard a woman shouting backstage. It was Little Bow Wow's mom getting onto him for not stopping and signing autographs for his fans. I mean this kid was maybe twelve years old, but his mom told him he needed to maintain his image. I couldn't help chuckling to myself.

Master P showed up totally unprepared, and we had to scramble to find even one of his tracks for him. My program director was pissed, but I couldn't get over how big of a presence we brought to this place with all these big rappers.

After the concert and the shock of being in this new world, it was time to get to work. Now I had to show what I could do in the booth, and I was determined to impress my new bosses.

CHAPTER 10.

Getting on air for the first time was an experience all on its own. Everyone listened to this radio station, especially young ladies who wanted to come see the DJs. The radio booth was like something off Star Trek, and behind me was a huge window where listeners would come up and try to impress the DJs so we would let them into the station for a minute to chat or maybe be on-air. I wish I could say I was a perfect angel, but I was eighteen and, one way or another, a lot of girls --mainly strippers -- found their way onto my nightly shows. The first night, some of those girls put on quite a show. When I asked if I would get in trouble for inviting them in, one of the senior DJs told me, "Have them come up and complete the window test. If they impress you and can make things interesting, you're doing yourself a favor." Most of the time my door was wide open during my shifts.

This one girl called my show and told me she was the hottest stripper in Vegas, so I invited her on my show. I had her strip live on the air, and I gave my listeners a play-by-play while she seduced me. This had everyone laughing and calling my show asking me who I was. This was one way to get the attention of my bosses and coworkers.

I started to be a mixture between Alan Berg and Howard Stern, two very influential DJs that I looked up to and leaned toward imitating on the radio. I felt a particular connection with Howard Stern because I'd seen his movie, Private Parts, and I knew he'd gone through similar things when he was starting out in radio. His wild sense of humor and creativity inspired many of my bits. Now remember, this was before social media -- the only thing we had was Myspace -- so the only way I could get negative comments was if someone called my boss and left an angry voicemail. During my shift, I pretty much had free reign to do or say what I wanted, and I always went to the limit.

I brought this personality with me every time I went to a club as well. On night I was at a club and happened to run into the biggest club DJ in Las Vegas. He was well-known around the country and could be found spinning live on-air one night a week. The first time I hosted his show, I had him almost on the floor laughing when I did Fear and Loathing impressions and chatted up women in between his breaks. Being on his good side came with perks. He had instant VIP access to anywhere in town, and I couldn't believe I was now his favorite DJ to be on-air with. The more I hosted his shows, the more access I got to Las Vegas.

The biggest club at the time besides RA at Luxor was Club Rain at the Palms. One night he told me to bring a guest and ask for a certain doorman. I didn't really know anybody at the time, so I went by myself. This guy walked me to a private elevator, and we went up three floors to the main DJ booth and VIP room. To think back now, not only was I eighteen and not even allowed to be in a casino, let alone the biggest club in Vegas, but I was also getting the red carpet to the top of the club with my own table and bottle service just because this club DJ liked me. I smiled, kept my mouth shut and just played the part, keeping my smug grin in check as I was being escorted past a crowd of people looking at me as if I were Leonardo DiCaprio getting ready to sign autographs.

Driving back to my apartment that night, I knew this is what

I wanted, and I was prepared to do anything it took to be full-time on-air and have a major daypart show. After that night, it became more tangible than ever.

I had always been good at competition. I don't know if it was just being hardheaded, but I was pretty sure I could compete with the best and win. Coming into one of the biggest radio stations in the country had its moments of nervousness, but that came with the job. I was a shock jock. Anything I could do to get a listener's attention in the first few seconds was fair game, and I was constantly working out new ways to stand out. I had contracted as a part timer, so I only had a few hours late at night to get as much tape as I needed to impress my bosses. They would listen back to my shows and breaks every week, typically giving me comments or critiques.

Although I had just two to three shows a week between three and five hours long, I took this as an opportunity to hone my craft. The more interaction I had with listeners the better, and I worked on cutting down the time I needed for a clean delivery. Radio stations were built on four main day parts: morning show, midday, afternoon, and nights. These shifts were five to six hours long, and only the top DJs at the time occupied them. This meant that there were a few short shifts between the regulars, and occasionally a part-timer would need to fill in if the main DJ was out. Besides me, there were around a dozen part-timers, so getting on air could be competitive.

Basically, I had to stand out, and my direct and sometimes outlandish approach would separate me from the rest. This was important when someone full-time took a day off and every part-timer had their hand up wanting to fill in. Since I was the new guy, I was the last one they thought of. This made my blood turn red. I wanted a chance to fill in. I sounded the best in my head, but there were other guys in front of me, and I had to be patient and show these guys I wanted it more.

After I had been on air in Vegas for a few months, I received a phone call from a TV talk show host in Chicago. They had heard about my story and wanted me on their show to talk with out-of-control children and motivate them to do better in life. This was out of the left field. Yes, I was out of control and maybe should have been in jail instead of being on-air in Las Vegas, but what did I have to say to these children? It meant publicity, and I was happy to share my story if people were interested, so I took advantage of the situation and jumped on a fully paid trip to Chicago.

Alright, maybe it wasn't the best choice to call up an old friend living in Chi Town and have him come by my suite and party all night before going on this talk show to tell teenagers to choose the right path in life. But this was my job now. The TV station had heard about me from a press release that I'd sent out for acting or modeling jobs in LA. This interview seemed like a great way to get a foot in the door. I showed up in Chicago like a rock star, jumping into a limo from the airport and getting a suite next to the John Hancock Building. I must have stayed up till three AM that night.

The next day at the studio, I was let into a room with ten kids and their parents. As we were waiting for our turn on set, I started telling them my story. I laugh about it now because I was trying to be as straightforward as possible and not show off my hangover too much. I did my best to be positive and motivational.

"Just because people say or think you're bad doesn't mean that's the way you will turn out. You choose your own destiny." Yeah, it was a bit cheesy, but I was doing my best and hoping I'd make a difference for these kids and maybe others watching at home.

As I was waiting for the real show to start, I witnessed something for the first time that made me sick to my stomach. The producers for this show had a live camera and were egging these kids on backstage, explaining to them how to act, for example, like they were smoking weed, laughing, and trying to make their parents cry. It was all for a show, and even though they were filming parts of the episode live, they were collecting footage to cut and make the show more sensational. It made me think how ridiculous it was to expect a wild party boy in Las Vegas to teach these kids how to straighten up and get their shit together.

The show ended up running late, and I never got my 30 seconds of fame, but some of the kids rode with me back to airport, and I got to talk one on one with them. I told them to take advantage of their independence, and if they wanted to do adult things, there was a level of responsibility that goes with that.

"Yes, I'm only eighteen with my own radio show, but I busted my ass to get here, and I never let anybody give me shit. I had to work and then work harder than the next guy to be given the spot that I have today."

Those kids showed me more about myself than anyone. It was more important than ever not to let the spotlight take over and derail me from my goal. I went back to Vegas with these things on my mind, and in a way, they helped remind me that I could do more for myself.

At this point, I had fallen into a normal routine. I had a one-bedroom apartment where I'd drag myself after a lot of late nights either at the station or out partying. I spent every hour I could at the radio station working with other DJs and voicing any advertising spots they gave me just to get voice out there.

I was a lonely kid; all my friends were back home and still in high school while I was out in the desert by myself most of the time. In my free time, I would go to nearby sport fields and kick footballs back and forth with myself, still thinking about kicking that winning field goal in the big game. Maybe I watched *Rudy* way too much, but for some reason, this was my release from everything.

I had always enjoyed movies, and now that I was alone, whenever I wasn't at work, I found myself watching every motivational movie possible. I hadn't gotten to a self-doubt spiral as low as the one I'd experienced in high school, but it wasn't always easy to stay positive. Watching films like *Rocky*, *Rudy or Private Parts* gave me a moment to think how great it would feel being on top and living in the moment. It helped to keep me motivated and think that one day I could have my own moment of glory.

I loved driving to LA, which was only three and a half hours from Vegas. I toyed with the idea of acting or modeling, thinking it would be a great direction to go if I ever gave up on radio. After graduation, one of my friends from back home moved out there trying to get a foot in the door for acting, and I stayed with her a couple times trying to look for auditions anywhere I could find them. I managed to get calls for a couple of MTV shows, but when they found out I was eighteen, they dropped me fast. Then I found a talent agency in Las Vegas casting for extras and small role positions. I sent in my resume thinking I would never hear back from them, but I got a voicemail a few days later asking if I could come by and audition for them.

I was on cloud nine. I must have run about twenty miles the night before the audition, and I was up early to make sure my outfit was perfectly pressed, and hair spiked to the nines. Of course, as big headed as I was, I thought this would be a one-on-one interview. Imagine my surprise when I arrived at this warehouse-style building where about two hundred people were waiting around for their chance to impress the agency. *Great.* I wasn't nervous. OK, maybe I was a little nervous, but I knew I had an advantage being an on-air DJ. I could impress whoever they put in front of me.

The witching hour chimed, and of course I was the first person they called up. There I was in front of two hundred wannabe actors, and I had to talk for a minute and half about myself to impress this agency. I had been psyching myself up, imagining that they were going to call me up first, but it was still surprising when it happened. I hit the stage talking myself up, just like I'd been doing on my radio show. I smiled and told everyone an amazing story about how I had been thrown out of high school but had gotten an internship on my local radio station, which had led to my on-air spot in Las Vegas.

When I made my way off stage and back to my seat, all I could think about was how stupid it was for me to compete with these actors. I really had no idea what I was doing there. Despite my doubts, I must have impressed someone. When I was done, one of the casting agents came up to me and asked if I would come into the other room for a minute. I walked into this empty room, and a man walked in.

"So, what are you doing for the next three days?"

"Whatever you would like me to do, sir." I replied.

"Good. Can you be at Caesars Palace at six AM?" asked the guy.

"Sure!" I was getting excited.

"George Clooney and Katherine Zeta Jones are filming a movie at the casino. You'll be a vacationer playing games behind them. We'll be happy to have you."

I saved my excitement for the car ride home and couldn't help calling everyone I knew to tell them what had just happened. I was learning at a young age that I'd only have seconds to impress somebody and get noticed, and this was something I had no problem doing.

CHAPTER 11.

Being an extra working on a movie set was not quite what I had been expecting. I had the idea I was going to have my own trailer, an assistant to get me coffee and some Hawaiian girl to fan me in between scenes. Perhaps real stars get that kind of treatment, but I was an extra, so they just put me into some dark closet with the other extras until they needed us. Sometimes we'd be in actual shots, but other times they just needed a body to stand in for hours while they worked on lighting or whatever was going on.

Then the surreal moment came. They called me out and paired me with a twenty-five-year-old hottie flight attendant as my wife, and we were gambling on the casino floor next to George Clooney for the next four hours while they shot this one scene. I couldn't help but notice Catherine Zeta Jones walking into the scene with this huge white poodle and the directors (Cohen Brothers) putting together this movie scene with me right in the middle of it. The next two days filming were one of the highlights of my life, but the real effect was the people I met there.

There was a guy a few years older than I was, who was a local comedian and industry worker. He got to know me and my story and told me to come by and hang out with him and some other wannabe comedians after the shoot. Leaving Caesars Palace and saying bye to George Clooney was awesome, but I was excited to meet some kids my own age who were already in the underground scene of Vegas and wanted to get to know me.

This group of young funny guys all hung out at a karaoke bar at the Stratosphere Hotel where they had a good time drinking and showing off for the casino guests. They welcomed me readily, and I spent many nights going up to sing classic songs and act out in hilarious ways just for a laugh and a free drink. One of the main guys in the comedy troop, Johnny Pot Roast, called me up on stage one night to act like a drunk guy with a lit cigarette in my mouth while he sang some Irish song. At the end, I faked passing out on stage and got a roaring response. I didn't have family out here or anybody I could really trust, but these guys treated me like one of their own, and in return, I lent my services any way I could. With my connections to the radio station, I always had perks like free tickets to shows, premieres and events. Although I knew they were impressed with my connections, I felt like they liked me for myself as well, and I started hanging with these guys every week.

I got used to being a part of comedy routines. These guys would perform at a local place called the Iowa Café and sometimes showrooms at local casinos. Before getting to know these guys, I had always thought of myself as something of a stand-up comedian; I mean every time I was on the radio, I was performing, so what would be the difference of doing it live and in-person? It turned out to be more challenging than I had anticipated.

My first opportunity to take the stage was at a comedy lounge off the Vegas Strip called the Beach. One of the members in the comedy troop got me in front of the director of the club for an audition. It was the first time in my life someone was asking me to be funny on the spot. I froze for a second, and then started doing a Chris Farley impression. I wasn't sure if I'd get in at first, but she started smiling and nodding, and I knew I had won her over. She told me she would be in contact to see if I could open for one of the bigger acts on the weekend.

I spent the next few days trying out impressions both on air and in private. I even stood in front of the mirror for hours at a time coming up with a skit that would work for tourists at this big comedy club. Finally, she contacted me and asked if I was ready to go, and of course I replied Yes.

I was psyching myself up bigtime all the way there, even playing Eminem's *Lose Yourself* on the car ride over and pumping myself up in the parking garage. This was the most nervous I had ever been in my life. It was worse than when I'd driven two thousand miles to somewhere where I knew nobody.

Walking into the club to see people in their seats made me want to throw up all over myself. I went to the MC and gave him an intro song for my act (Scatman), then headed backstage to get ready. My heart was pounding. I was the first one to go on, of course. When they announced my name, I ran up to the stage like a cannon shot, grabbed the microphone, and completely forgot what I was going to say.

This was not my best moment. The only thing that came to mind was to do a Chris Farley impression and chug the pitcher of beer I had the bartender grab me. I was so embarrassed. I relapsed to acting like Matt Foley, the motivational speaker, and asking random people in the crowd, "What do you want to do with your life?" I finished fast and ran off stage thinking this was the worst performance ever done in the history of comedy.

To my surprise, the manager thought it was funny and called me the next day to invite me back for another performance. What? In my head, I figured this was the worst show ever, but someone thought it was funny. Of course, I said yes and scheduled another show for the next month. I called my family back home laughing, but I was glad the manager thought it was funny.

I kept practicing, and I used my radio audience for feedback on what jokes to tell and what impressions I should do. I got tons of calls and fan support. The next time, I would be ready.

Since I was only working part time, I had a lot of free time from the radio station. I thought I was doing well for myself, especially as I was spending extra time with my comedy friends thinking up ways to be funny. I got a lot of feedback from my bosses, and a lot of it was good. Any day now, I expected to get a bigger chunk of the available airtime.

Every week the boss would post the schedule on his office door. I usually wasn't surprised to see that my hours hadn't increased, but one time there was a big opening because one of the DJs was out of town. I felt I had a good shot at getting onto the daytime slot. I guess I got my hopes up a bit too high, though. Normally when I saw the same old wimpy schedule, I'd walk away disappointed, but this time I wasn't having it. Over the next week, I was scheduled for only two shows, both three hours each, and I was not happy. I went back to the DJ lounge, found a sharpie, circled my air shifts, and wrote "I'M PISSED OFF!" right across the schedule.

The next morning, my phone rang awfully early.

"Hello?" I tried to sound more awake than I felt.

"This is the station manager. You'll report to my office as soon as possible."

He hung up. *Well, this is it, I'm getting fired today.* Driving to the station, I couldn't stop beating myself up for having done something so stupid. What did I think was going to happen? Was I supposed to get a reward for being whiny?

I knocked hesitantly, and when he invited me in, I slunk to a seat in front of his massive desk.

"I almost fired you this morning," he started. I struggled to look at him for a moment before he continued, "But I thought of myself and what I would have done at your age so couldn't blame you. You do realize you're our newest hire, right? There are people who have been here for years and have more experience than you, and I'll always respect that. Understood?"

I fought down my frustration and replied humbly, "I understand. I'm ready for more shifts, and I won't do this kind of thing again."

"Just hang tight, kid. You'll get there."

I took a big breath. "Thank you for not firing me."

"Keep it up on the air. Your personality does well on your show, but I don't need that kind of attitude around the office. You keep doing well, and I'll see what I can do to get you more shifts."

I felt very grateful at that moment, and from then on out it was "yes sir" and "what can I do, sir" when I was around him. I had already impressed him on-air. Now I needed to show him my work ethic.

Thanks to some hard work, I was still doing solid airshifts, and I began to get more recognition around the radio station. More and more shifts started to come.

Just like in my hometown, I was making demo tapes on every show and producing all my own commercials, but I was still part-time. Demo tapes were basically my best shows all mixed down to a two-minute audio tape. This was my resume, how I got to Vegas, and I knew I would have to let my bosses hear it so I could move up in the lineup. However, this was hard to do; a full-time position opened up about once in five years. It was branding for the radio station, and they wanted to have DJs that were live every day so the ratings would go up and the station would stay number one throughout the year. I realized that I wasn't getting full-time anytime soon, and I really didn't have any experience to show off to them besides my old station and Vegas.

Now, every DJ needs to take a break from time to time, so I was waiting for one of the big guys to leave for a few days and give me an opportunity. The biggest daypart was the afternoon, prime time, and the biggest DJ, who was also the assistant PD, naturally had the spot. When this guy took a vacation, every part timer prayed. Now, the assistant PD hated me, and he was anal about how things were executed. I was shocked when I got the call and they wanted me, the part time night shock jock, to come in and fill the biggest vacancy on the station for one afternoon.

It was a Friday show, and I came out firing. Every break was money to me, and I came up with a great show prep idea: Big Black Beautiful Friday! Every caller I put on the air was a big black girl, and it was a celebration to them. I had them laughing, crying, and wanting more after every call. I was turning heads throughout the radio station for being so bold and creative. This was a golden show, and I recorded all of it. Later, I enjoyed piecing it together for the new demo reel I was putting together.

Come Monday morning, my phone was ringing at an ungodly hour again.

"Come into the boss's office. He wants to see you."

I was sweating the whole drive there, thinking about the last stunt I'd pulled, sure that I'd really be fired this time.

Once again, I crept into the PD's office, unsure what the reception would be.

"The assistant program director is very pissed off," he said by way of greeting. I gulped. "He's been getting complaint calls about you all morning." I closed my eyes, waiting for the axe, but instead he said, "This is great. If they're calling here, that means they are listening. Keep doing what you're doing."

My frown turned into a smile fast, and I realized the man was complimenting my ability to gain an audience's attention.

When I left the PD's office, the assistant program director caught me in the hallway to give me his two cents, ending by telling me I had no future at the station. "You can never get full-time here, kid, no matter what shit you pull on air. The positions open once every ten years, and it's almost impossible for you to move up. Try something else." But I couldn't have cared less. This guy was overrated, and I knew I had my boss's attention. I walked a little bit taller that day, and I didn't let anyone get in my way.

The next week was my second time on the comedy stage, and I needed a boost after my lame first performance. I showed up to the club early and started drinking at the bar, getting my spirits up. I was a few drinks in when I looked over and noticed someone who seemed familiar to me. She looked just like my grandmother. I almost choked on my drink in shock, but I realized quickly that this couldn't be her. This woman had brown hair, and my grandmother was a blonde. Besides, my grandmother was in Florida, two thousand miles away. I shook my head and just focused on rehearsing my lines for the comedy skit.

After a few vodkas and cranberries, I was ready for the show. This time I did a lot better. I didn't forget everything I'd been planning on saying, for once, and I was able to keep up the energy throughout the skit. I got a positive response for the short time I was up there, and I was able to grin as I left the stage.

I went back to the bar and ordered another drink. To my surprise, the woman from earlier was waiting for me. With a flourish, she pulled off her hair, revealing familiar blonde locks.

"Hi," she said, and this time there was no mistaking her for anyone else. It was my grandmother. "Are you surprised?" she grinned. It turned out she had flown out here in secret and had been enjoying a vacation in Vegas while she waited for the perfect time to sneak up to me. I almost broke down in tears as I hugged her very tight and said thank you for coming.

Her support reminded me of all the people I had back at home who were rooting for me. I was doing this for them in a way. I couldn't go back a failure. There was no time to lose, and now it was on.

CHAPTER 12.

I turned nineteen and was still just part time, waiting for a spot to open up. I volunteered for any shift I could get. and I spent a lot of time with the street team doing live promotions for the radio station all over town. After more and more airchecks and my bosses telling me how good I was doing, I was getting restless. I knew I had what it would take to be full time, but the PD was comfortable with his current lineup, and nobody was leaving any time soon.

One day I was looking online for full-time radio jobs around the country and saw a posting in East Tennessee. There was a new hip hop station looking for all day parts and a new nighttime DJ. I felt like my current position wasn't getting me anywhere, so I emailed my demo to the new program director, not thinking I would get a call back. But I did.

They were looking for a full-time night DJ to host the six to eleven pm show and would pay for moving expenses to get there. This was a hard decision; I was just getting my name out there in Vegas, but this radio station in Knoxville was ready to move me across the country and pay for everything so I could be their new nighttime DJ. I couldn't make this decision by myself, so I asked the closest person to me, my program director, for advice.

"Nah, that's not where you want to be. It's a good job, sure, but that guy is an asshole. I'd wait for another position. I can help you find something better."

I wasn't sure what to do, but I realized CBS Vegas wouldn't hire me full time without more experience. I had to decide. I spent a few days mulling it over, and finally I went back into his office and told him I was taking the position. I knew he would respect me in the end for going to Tennessee because he knew where I wanted to be full-time in Vegas.

The next day I signed a contract to be the new nighttime DJ in Knoxville, TN. I was only nineteen, and here I was moving across the country again. I convinced myself that this was an opportunity I could not pass up. I needed the experience. As I mentioned, one of my role models was Howard Stern, and I'd learned from his film, *Private Parts*, that one way to make it big was to take any job that was better than the one he had. I was determined to do better for myself, so I packed up everything I owned into a moving truck and printed out MapQuest directions.

I still can't believe I made it across the states twice without GPS. Facebook wouldn't be invented for a few years yet, so I didn't even have a way to share this amazing journey or find a couch to crash on as I went along. This was the first time I had driven so far alone, and that was nerve wracking. But in radio, I'd had to do a lot by myself, and as much as I was a celebrity on the radio, I still lived alone in my head. I thought about everything on that drive: life, girls, this new town I was going to, everything. It was excited and terrified all in one, but all I could do was drive.

Pulling into East Tennessee was like driving back to my small hometown. This time people knew who I was and were excited to have me there. My new program director had me meet him at a country western bar near the college campus -- he would be the only black guy and the only one not wearing cowboy boots. I found myself walking into an urban cowboy hell. The PD introduced himself and welcomed me to my new city. He looked like a typical radio geek, not some flashy night jock or funny morning show guy, just a nerd.

"Well, you made the right choice by hiring me," I told him. "I will do anything and everything I can to get people listening." He grinned, eager to get started.

Now I was working on my third radio show in my third state with a bunch of weight on my shoulders. My PD was new to this town as well. This was one of the first Top 40 hip hop radio stations in East Tennessee, which was a pretty big change from the country and gospel stations that had saturated the airwaves up to that point. The PD left me alone, informing me that they had reserved a hotel room near the station for me till I found my own apartment. I finished up my drink, two-stepped with some blonde country girl and headed over the hotel.

As much of a dream as this would be for anyone in my position, the moment I opened the hotel room door to see the banner and gift boxes arranged for my arrival, I fell to the floor in tears. What had I done now? The loneliness hit me just like it had on my first night in Vegas, and I felt like I was drowning in depression. This time there was no George to pull me back onto my feet.

Don't get me wrong: I was ready to show my talents and jump on the air, but it was just me, my rental truck, and this hotel room in the middle of nowhere. I kept hearing my mother's words, "If you come home, we will be doing the same thing tonight and every night after that. There's nothing here for you." I kept repeating that over and over in my head as I watched *Rudy* some twenty times that night and tried to pump myself up and get my head where it needed to be.

The next day I went to the radio station and met my new crew. These guys were rednecks and good ole country folk, nothing like the crew in Vegas. I was pretty much the top dog. The PD was my boss of course, and there was a midday guy, but other than that, everyone else was either inexperienced or part time. They were excited I was there. They listened eagerly to my audition tape and fell over laughing at some of my demos. They couldn't wait for me to pop the mic.

Everything was brand new in the building. Walking into the radio booth for the first time, I felt like a new heavyweight walking into boxing ring, determined and ready. My first night on the air I had all the phone lines lit up and my new boss giving me thumbs up through the glass. I didn't just impress them; I made them laugh, and even the bosses wanted to hear more. I think I made up a contest to see how many girls in Knoxville would call, and I convinced my PD to let me do more giveaways whenever I got up to a certain number. I was more flirting with their country accents than anything, but my show sounded solid, and it was a good start for this new move.

I stayed in that hotel for a week, and that was enough for me. A salesgirl at the radio station I had flirted with since day one drove me around, and I found an apartment in the one of the newest complexes in town. To my surprise, my new neighbor downstairs was from Florida as well. He was my age and was going to college down the street. This guy made me feel at home. Not only did we have inside jokes about home, but he was mesmerized by my stories from Vegas and all my radio shows. Every time we partied at his place or mine, it was total frat boy college partying. If we weren't pulling girls from local clubs, we were partying on campus at University of Tennessee. I guess I left Vegas, but Vegas hadn't left me.

My first couple of months on-air in Knoxville brought a lot of attention to the radio station. Radio advertisement was going up, live appearances and endorsement were being booked all over the place, and I was starting to feel accepted by this new place as I built my show for my new listeners. Despite all that attention, I still spent a lot of time by myself. Besides partying, I was pretty much a loner. Just like in Vegas, I would go to parks and kick footballs for hours at a time, still thinking maybe one day I could run out of a tunnel and be some big football star. When it wasn't that, I was spending a lot of time updating my audition tapes. Even as I polished my Knoxville show, I couldn't help but imagine myself back in Vegas, this time with my own full-time show.

Eventually, the station hired one of the biggest club DJs in town, and I spent many nights with him and my newly acquired club gig. I would broadcast my show every Friday night, and he would play music in between my breaks. I walked into that club like John Travolta in Saturday Night Fever every week. I mean, it wasn't Vegas, but I liked to think I could still carry this persona and make everyone I put on the air feel like a celebrity.

This was the perfect radio job for anyone in 2003: small town celebrity and anything I wanted was right there at my feet. I made some solid friends there and enjoyed a vibrant nightlife that only a college town can offer. At the radio station, things couldn't have been better. Every show I did was just as good as the last one, and I had a regular following despite my show being under a year old.

Then, one day I heard that a new hip hop station was opening in town. My coworkers couldn't shut up about it, and from what I could tell, it was owned by the biggest radio station in Knoxville. When I heard the news, I immediately ran out to the radio station vehicle and made my way over to the competitor to show them who was the boss.

This radio truck was fully loaded. Sure, it was 2004, but we had everything from fifteen-inch speakers with dueling subwoofers and all the latest in sound blasting. So, I made my move: I drove the station vehicle over to the rival station and played "Trill Ville Neva Eva" as loud as the speakers would go with my ass hanging out the window. I figured I'd show them that our station was ready for radio war while challenging them with my own version of "I'm ready to play; show me what you got!"

I didn't mean any harm, but apparently some people thought this was crossing a line. One of my coworkers in particular caught me as I got back from my trip across the street and immediately berated me for being an immature jerk, making us look bad, and losing our advertising dollars. I hadn't started out with the intention of being an arrogant prick, but in the face of this lecture, I had no choice but to puff up my chest and defend myself. I felt justified when I found my boss laughing his ass off and congratulating me.

It's hard to explain to anyone who has never had a radio show or been in the spotlight that I had to make my presence known. This was just a part of the gig. I didn't have a life; radio was my life. I did nothing but focus on my show and make sure that every night was better than the last. If social media had been around in 2004, I would have been thrown under the bus every day for the things that came out of my mouth. If I wasn't saying vulgar things to women and running lesbian pick-up games on the air, I wasn't doing my job.

When I got back from my little stunt, the verbal lashing this coworker in marketing gave me was just enough to tip me over. I had only been in Knoxville for a little over a year, but we had already hit #2 in the market. I had the following and support, but enough was enough.

I honestly regret what I did next. I should have had a more

democratic approach to this situation and taken some time to think about it, but I didn't give a fuck. I marched into the operations manager's office and demanded that my coworker be reprimanded for interfering with my show and stunt. I was the talent, and she was just along for the ride.

The operations manager was very concerned over my complaint and pulled both of us into the office to resolve the situation. I told him, "I want this person fired. We should all be on the same team and supportive of getting to number one in the market at any means possible. If she doesn't see it that way, I can't work with her."

The operations manager did not see it my way. "I will not be letting her go."

"Hell, either you fire her, or I'm gone, and I'm taking my show with me."

A word of advice on giving ultimatums; this is a fine line and it's easy to go too far. When you do something like this in life, you must be ready to handle the outcome. In this situation, I was wrong, and I let my emotions get the best of me. The operations manager sighed and said, "Nobody is getting fired. Everyone here needs to do their part to get along. Sure, there are conflicts sometimes, but we can work through this." But this wasn't me. I was sure in that moment that I was right, and the operations manager was being dumb. I let my pride take over my reasoning. The next day I made a decision. I walked into the boss's office and resigned from my position, telling them I would not bow down to anyone. Then I left.

CHAPTER 13.

I was heartbroken, but I hadn't gotten started in radio to kiss ass and be a team player. I know this sounds egotistical and immature but remember that was radio. It was my job to put everything out there, no holding back. I used my personality as fuel to attract people to my show, and I couldn't stand feeling like someone was putting a leash on me.

I regretted this decision immediately after I left the station. I walked away feeling like I had failed. Not only was this one of the first hip hop radio stations in East Tennessee, but I had become the second highest rated night DJ in town. I had been at the top of the of my game, but I walked away from it because of my pride. Now I had nothing.

In a fury, I rented a U-Haul and packed up my entire apartment. I knew I was making the biggest mistake of my life. Not only was I not on the air anymore, but I was leaving everything I had worked so hard for. I had even left Vegas for this opportunity, and here I was with absolutely nothing to show for it.

Not knowing what else to do, I turned toward the only place I knew I could take a minute to think and figure out my next step: back home. I called my hometown radio station and talked to my former boss to let him know what had happened. He told me to come back; they would put me on the air immediately.

"Look, everything is going to be OK. These things happen.

You've just got to move on. You still have loads of opportunities ahead of you, so try not to worry about it."

This was hard to hear because everything in my head was telling me that I had fucked up royally. How could I have left my biggest opportunity in Vegas only to ruin everything in Tennessee? But hey, I'd started this journey with nothing, so really, I hadn't lost anything. Sometimes in life, you fall down, and you have to get up and start over.

Going home turned out to be the perfect way to unwind. It was great to see all my old friends and coworkers and be back in the radio station that I'd grown up in. This is where it had all started, and I was welcomed with open arms. For a few days I enjoyed being a big fish in a small pond, but after a while, I knew I would never be happy doing this. I had been on my way to the top in Vegas and I just needed a bit more experience to really dazzle the big guns. My self-doubt over the Knoxville disaster kept me from moving for a long time though, and I just kept on going at it on my home radio station, rocking it on the airwaves.

I looked everywhere I could for the motivation I knew I needed to get back into the game. I wasn't even 21 yet, and I had already accomplished so much. I sometimes drove to the high school I had been kicked out of and would sit in the parking lot trying to boost my ego by remembering how great it had felt when they had called me back, but it still wasn't enough. I wanted that full-time position in Vegas, but I just wasn't sure I could get there.

When I needed a break from my thoughts, I would go kick footballs and drive past Florida State Doak Campbell stadium, still thinking I had the balls to try out for the football team and one day run out on that field. I was a dreamer, but I knew I had enough ice in my blood to do anything I wanted. I was in control of my own destiny.

I was on the air at my home station several days a week, and I figured it was good practice for when I went back to a bigger studio. I spent countless hours at the radio station improving my shows and making demo tapes, and when I worked up the nerve, I began sending my stuff out to any station that was accepting full-time applications. I got offers from Green Bay, Dallas, and little towns here and there, but nothing that got my attention. It didn't matter though; I was comfortable in my hometown and enjoyed being on-air there.

In December 2004, I was finally turning twenty-one. I would finally be old enough to be legally allowed in all the places I'd been partying for the past few years. I wanted this birthday to be like no other. My best friend growing up would also be celebrating his birthday that same week, so we decided to celebrate together and book a cruise. It was now six months after the Knoxville tragedy, and I was looking forward to taking a break from life and jumping on that boat. After all that time working and traveling, I had the chance to spend a week just being a kid in a sombrero in the middle of Mexico.

I did a lot of soul searching on that trip in between taking tequila shots and partying with the local hotties. This was the break I needed. It reminded me of all the good memories I'd made as a Vegas playboy, and when it was over, I didn't want to get off that boat. It made me think, and I realized I was just playing a role. The past few months I hadn't been doing what I needed to do to get what I really wanted: my own Vegas show. After that cruise ended, I said enough was enough. I needed to take another chance and do what I had set out to do in the first place. I made up my mind to drop everything and just go back out west.

After all this time, the assistant program director's words kept rattling around in my head. He'd told me that it was impossible for me to get a full-time spot in Vegas. Well, nobody was going to tell me what I could or couldn't do in life.

After celebrating New Year's at home, I let my listeners know that I was moving back out to Vegas and chasing my dreams of having a prime time show on the radio. This was almost turning into a joke for some people, and I'm sure there were bets out on how long it would be before I had failed and was back again. However, I didn't care what anybody said. I was on a mission, and this was my time. I had so much to prove to everyone who had ever doubted me--teachers, co-workers and even family. But I had more to prove to myself than anything.

Before I left, I made sure that I had a place to live. I didn't want to go all out and get my own place and come out to Vegas like some big shot. I sold everything; all my furniture, all my toys, everything had to go. This was a new beginning, just like when I had left for Vegas the first time. Instead of getting a nice apartment, I arranged a place to live with one of my former coworkers. Then I threw a few suitcases into my car and left.

As I started again on this journey, I could only think about what everyone in my life had been telling me since I was a kid. "You will never be smart enough for school." "You will never do anything worthwhile." "Your bad attitude will make you a failure." I thought about my mother, who had done her best to support me even while she went through shit. I thought of my father, who I hadn't seen again since I was in high school. I thought of my teachers and coworkers and all the other people who had given up on me or told me I'd never make it. I wanted to turn all these negatives into a positive.

I drove straight through, stopping only for gas. I bought a footlong sub sandwich in Pensacola and finished it by the time I was in Texas. By then, my mind was fixed on the single thought of getting back to the radio station in Vegas and begging for my old job. The scenery rushed by, starting with the beaches and the ocean breeze in Florida and transforming to the flat and rugged landscape of Texas. In Houston I decided to keep going southwest through to El Paso and then up through New Mexico and Arizona. I drove all night and all day without a break except for a few hours of sleep at a truck stop outside Deming, NM.

On my death bed I will still remember what it was like to see Vegas coming into view from the mountain. I passed Kingman, AZ and headed through Boulder City and the Hoover Dam. The best time to see Vegas is at night when the city seems like a glittering jewel surrounded by darkness. As I drove through twists and turns over and through the mountains with nothing in sight but sand and darkness, I began to see a glow off in the distance. The first thing that caught my eye was the Stratosphere Hotel and then the Luxor with that shining light piercing through the clouds.

This time I didn't have to ask myself what I had done. Even though I had just left everything behind me and driven out to Las Vegas on nothing but a dream, I knew this was where I wanted to be. I pulled into town around midnight and rolled around Las Vegas Blvd. I told myself I was here to finish what I'd started.

My first day back at the radio station wasn't what I'd expected. I knew I would have to have a humble approach just showing up, but the last time I'd been here, I'd gotten used to the red-carpet treatment. Surely, they'd welcome me with open arms, right? Wrong. Just like before, they didn't have room for another DJ, and since they'd replaced me two years ago, there wasn't a single open spot in the studio, not even part time.

This was a major setback, and to be honest, I was thrown back. I had thought that with my resume and experience both here and in Knoxville, I was guaranteed a job. Instead, I had to beg the PD to give me any little crumb, and he only reluctantly agreed to give me fill in shifts and part time when needed. I didn't care. I was so grateful for the opportunity to be on-air at the number one hip hop station in Vegas, I didn't care if they gave me three hours a week, I was going to take it.

I ran out of that station like I had just been offered a million-dollar contract: I was back on the air in Vegas, and nothing else mattered. That night I was back on the Strip enjoying VIP access and free drinks. The DJs in Vegas were treated like kings, and that night everyone went all out to welcome me back to the party scene. Now, don't get me wrong; I wasn't a full-time DJ like I had been in Knoxville, but I was with my old crew, and they were happy to have me. This was Las Vegas, and when we walked into a club, we did it in style. These were the biggest nightclubs in the world, and they wanted us there every night so we would go back and talk about it on the radio. This was something that nobody else had. I breezed past bigtime celebrities who were stuck waiting for tables, and when they got them, they were sitting in the small booths next to ours.

Being a part-time DJ and fill in jock for the biggest radio station in Las Vegas was quite a bit different than what I'd gotten used to as a full-time jock in Knoxville. I always got the worst time spots, and if I wanted to increase my hours, I had to be willing to do what the bigger DJs didn't want to do. If my boss called me at 3AM to ask me to come in, you bet I'd be hauling ass to make it in on time. It didn't matter if somebody didn't show up for an airshift and I needed to show up to set up for a six am live broadcast or if the station needed promotion street team members to hand out stickers and support listeners for an event we were doing, I would do anything and everything for the radio station. I tried to always be the first one there. I didn't have much going for me -- no college degree, only a few years of experience, and I was the lowest guy on the totem pole. All I had was determination and willpower, so I made the best of it and worked hard to let these guys know that I would be the first and only person they needed to rely on.

The first person to make me realize that I was worth it and had a shot at being a full-time DJ was a sales guy from New York named Joey. This guy was the biggest and hottest sales guy in the business, and we made a connection the first time we met in person. Not only was he smart when it came to sales, but if anyone knew radio and the money that could be made from a top-rated show, it was this guy. One morning, some morning-show guy was making fun of me in the hallway for being from the south. As this guy was making a redneck joke, NY Joey stepped in and gave it right back to him. He made fun of the guy's lazy eye and bad haircut. NY Joey and I were pretty good friends from there on. It turned out he had been listening to my show, and I was able to turn to him for pointers and suggestions. He had been around the block and was overall a great guy to hang out with.

I was feeling good at this point. Hey, I was just a part-time nobody, but everyone at the radio station knew that if they needed anything, I was the guy to call. I proved myself even more reliable one night when I got an email around midnight asking if any part-timers were available for a set-up and broadcast for a music video at the Venetian Hotel and Casino with Ginuwine. I was the first one to respond, "YES."

Sure enough, I got a response right away: "Get down there at 6 AM and make it happen." I'd never been so glad I was always checking my emails at odd hours. This was another chance for me to impress the bosses, and I was ready to go.

I didn't know exactly what I was going to be doing except for live breaks and maybe an interview of the artist in the video, but it was more than that. The producer for the shoot invited me to sit with him while they set up the lights and got ready to film. This was awesome. For a minute, everyone on set took me for someone who oversaw picking which of the hot girls got to stand in front of the camera. The whole experience was awesome because some part of me still wanted to get into acting. Plus, this was being filmed at one of my favorite bars, the V Bar at Venetian. I did a spectacular interview with Ginuwine and Baby, making the bosses proud once again. Going back to the V Bar a few nights later was like being on top of the world.

CHAPTER 14.

In May 2005 I was still living in the same apartment with a co-worker and working like a madman. My time at the station was almost frenzied at times, but I had the run of the town when I wasn't working or sleeping. It was NY Joey and me running the street. We knew all the right guys, so I'd just make a call or send a text and tell my inside person that I was coming and how many friends, and I was pretty much guaranteed access to the DJ booth or first available table. That's all it took. We didn't need money or girls. I was on the air, so they took care of me like I was gold.

I became a master at finding an in at these places. I would get random phone calls from people that knew someone who'd gotten my number from someone in Florida and wanted to go out in Vegas for a night. If I was in a good mood, I would entertain them and show them Vegas. I remember one time I got a call from another DJ in South Carolina. His girlfriend was in town and wanted to be taken out. How could I say no? She turned out to be smoking hot. I picked her up from her hotel and took her to the hottest club in town, Club Rain at the Palms Casino. The streets were packed, so we started at Studio 54 at MGM Grand and then headed toward the Palms. I was all over this girl trying to show her the VIP ropes and all the power I got for being a part-time DJ. When we were leaving the club, I spotted someone that looked familiar. It was Scott Caan from Varsity Blues. Caan's father was in Godfather and Elf, and Scott himself was a big actor. I rolled down my window and said, "Hey, bro, where are you going?"

"I'm heading to the gas station for cigarettes and aspirin for my friend."

"I'll give you a ride." He grinned and popped into the back seat. My girl was totally flirting with him the whole time. I told him this was a bad neighborhood, so I'd take him to a gas station and drop him off at his hotel. I never asked him for his autograph, but he could just as well have asked for mine. At that point, with my connections, if you needed anything or to get in anywhere in Vegas, I was the person you wanted to know.

Yet all of this seemed pitiful without a full-time radio show. At the end of the day, I was just a wannabe nobody. I started looking at different offers. I even spent a few days in Fresno, CA for an interview. I wanted to further my career, and Vegas was looking like the place where that wasn't going to happen. Yes, I had the biggest connections, and NY Joey and I were on the prowl when it came to clubs and meeting celebrities, but I was thinking about my future in radio, and all the perks was starting to be bigger than I was. I mean, who cares that I was busting my ass at the radio station if no one was taking notice? I wanted more, and I started looking for better opportunities, even if it meant leaving radio.

The universe works in mysteries ways, and in May 2005, something impossible happened. All this time I had been riding the coattails of others and living the dream without actually being in the main spotlight or accomplishing my goals. One morning I woke up and checked my work schedule online just like I would any other day. I saw that I had gotten an email telling me to come in to the operations manager and program director's office for an urgent update to the staff and schedule. Now, in the radio business there was no way this was a good email. It meant one of two things: either the radio station was switching formats and going in a different direction with programming and staff, or I was getting fired.

I was nervous. That was longest ride into the station of my life. Walking down the hallway to the boss's office, I heard of conversation about a DJ who was leaving, and my heart sank as I realized they were probably talking about me. I made a point of catching a few people's eyes since this might be the last time I got to see them as a coworker.

I walked into office and saw all three of my big bosses and the general manager for the radio station, who I don't think even knew my name before that morning.

My PD spoke up. "So, one of our long time DJs is moving on to another career. We need to fill his full-time position. Although we considered bringing in another talent from a different radio station, we also reviewed your work and decided you might be a good fit. Is that something you'd be interested in?"

I tried not to get emotional in front of these guys who I had spent four years trying to impress. "Absolutely," I said without hesitation. This was the closest feeling I have ever come to something like winning the lottery. For once, I had nothing else to say.

This shouldn't have happened to someone like me. I was just that kid who had blown in with a big ego and a chip on his shoulder from all the people who hadn't believed in him. This was the best form of revenge I could have asked for: success. I drove about 150 miles per hour to the strip playing Ram Jam Black Betty and went out to party as the new full-time late-night DJ in Las Vegas, NV, and partied like a rock star. I went all out: limos, drinking, and all of my friends were invited.

I started work shortly after, bringing out the persona I had been refining over the past four years, Lumpy the BoyToy. I pulled out all the stops and went at it 110%. My first few air shifts were a live freak show, and I had every listener in Vegas calling me up, congratulating me and welcoming me to the late-night world of Vegas. I had celebrities, strippers, vampires, you name it. I did it, and they listened.

My new counterpart on the show was NY Joey. Now that I was full time, he had something to sell, and he was up to the challenge. With his publicity, I found myself more popular than ever. I was getting my own club gigs at some of the biggest casinos on the strip. I started doing live broadcasts from Mandalay Bay, the Venetian and Caesars Palace. I was making more money in live broadcasts and endorsements than anyone else at the radio station, and my listeners couldn't get enough of me. If there was a party or new club in Las Vegas in 2005, I was the host, and everyone who was anyone wanted to be there with me. One of my big club gigs was Pure Nightclub at Caesars Palace. It was common for local entertainers and celebrities to stop by. Carrot Top and Chris Angel were some of my regulars.

On one night, I found out Mike Tyson was going to be there, and I knew I had to try to get an interview and plug live on the air that he was going to be in the club. I got my VIP table all ready and waited to see his entourage so I could try to grab him for a minute. In these situations, with high profile celebrities, they would make their way by the regular VIP tables, usually surrounded by security or groupies, and then head off to a private table or room where they'd disappear for the rest of the night. Catching them on their way there was the only way to secure an interview, but I was prepared. As Tyson was walking in with about four bodyguards, I grabbed my wireless mic, told my producer I was going to grab him and walked up to his security guard. I think at first, he thought I was just a fan. "Fuck off," he said, reaching to shove me aside.

I showed him my microphone, "I'm with CBS Las Vegas. Does Mike have a few words for the night show?" The guard glanced at Tyson, who recognized me and my crew thanks to the banner.

"Sure, no problem." He grabbed the mic and gave me what I still consider the best twenty-second interview I've ever done. "Hi, it's Mike Tyson. Hello to all the local Vegas listeners. Come down to Caesars and hang out at Pure!" Then he handed the mic back and went on to his private lounge.

I was happier than ever. I'd had Iron Mike Tyson on my show, and my confidence in pulling in those big interviews built my credibility even more with the radio station. If there was anybody who would take chances like that, it was going to be me. You know the movie The *Hangover*? Every night was like that for me; yes, even that scene with the bed falling out of the suite. This was my life, and the craziness that happened to the film characters over two days happened to me every night. Sometimes I would look from the rooftop bar at Caesars and think about how much I wanted to entertain all these people. I had done it. I was living the dream.

CHAPTER 15.

In the early 2000s, people didn't have smart phones or social media. Instead, they listened to the radio, and in Vegas, that meant they were listening to me. Besides partying seven days a week, I was getting paid to be this loud personality on the radio, and I did my job as best as I knew how. My goal was to make you think, *what will he say next?* or *Oh my gosh, I can't believe he just said that.* I didn't know any other way, and I found myself improving this talent to separate myself from the others.

To be honest, I didn't like radio DJs. They all sounded the same to me, and I didn't want to come off like I was giving away a cheap prize on some game show. To me, radio was a theatre of the mind, and I put my own spin on that with dirty jokes and a cocky delivery. This is why the big bosses had me in their corner; I was the late-night relief in a world of cookie cutter DJs. I put in the extra hours and worked on the overall image of my show so that it would be like no other.

The station's biggest contest prize of the year was a fully paid Mexico cruise with all the DJs, and it was the hottest ticket in town. To get on this boat, a listener had to go through a whole orchestrated event and win a golden ticket. It was always a great time, and that year, I was more excited than ever. As the nighttime DJ, I oversaw one of the buses that went to Los Angeles where the cruise ship would start. I got on the bus in Vegas early in the morning ready to party. By the time we got there, I had to be carried on the ship like a complete moron singing the *Love Boat* theme and asking everyone where Gopher was. Most of my listeners had never seen my face, and I felt like a total celebrity. What a great impression I made wearing a captain's hat and three sheets to the wind. I'm surprised nobody got pregnant or died on that boat. On the second night I ended up in someone's suite half naked with a sombrero and a bottle of tequila. I mean, it wasn't a full-blown party until the DJ gets naked and starts singing Mexican songs till four in the morning.

After we got back off the boat, it was business as normal: back to the radio station and back to being the late-night freak I'd groomed myself to be. I had become the second most listened late-night DJ in Las Vegas. I would start off every show with a fully produced disclaimer intro: "Lock up your daughters and wives: it's time for Lumpy the Boytoy! Fasten your seat belt, and strap in, bitch; it's going to be a wild ride." I took pride in making all my own intros and sound effects so that it would sound like the biggest and freakiest show anyone had ever heard.

As 2007 rolled in, I started hearing about this new popular website, Facebook. The only thing I knew about it was that users could use it to reconnect with old friends. I wasn't really excited about it. I mean, nobody knew what social media was yet. I figured if you could have friends on the internet, why not have a friend named Lumpy the BoyToy? To me, the whole Facebook thing was just that: a thing; my show was real and always new and interesting.

One day everything changed. One Monday in 2007, I received an email calling all DJs and radio station staff into a meeting that would not only change me but everyone in the industry. I walked into the conference room at the radio station with a lump in my throat and took a seat alongside my nervous coworkers. The program director put a piece of paper in front of us all. It was a news article about a DJ in New York. I recognized the guy from my old station in Florida, though apparently, he had moved on to bigger and better things. Until today, that is. Apparently, this DJ had posted a bunch of inappropriate pictures on his social media page featuring young boys and himself with radio station logos all over the place. The entire industry was freaking out. Of course, everyone was appalled -- I mean, how disgusting -- but now the radio stations were nervous. The FCC was fining the New York station and the DJ for inappropriate behavior and had apparently become trigger happy, sending out warnings to stations all over the country for inappropriate and vulgar behavior associated with the radio station. Well, inappropriate and vulgar was how I started my show every night. I didn't know any other way, and this was how I made my living.

After the meeting, the big bosses pulled me in the office and sat me down to talk about my show. This wasn't good, and I could tell they wanted to have a serious conversation. So far we hadn't run into any trouble, and I always put out a solid broadcast, but they didn't want the whole station to go down because of something I said. I wasn't about to change my style of radio just because some idiot in New York got into trouble. They told me they wanted to keep everything clean and to cut back on the certain stunts and visitors I was having on my shows. I wasn't allowed to do the same phone skits with women or talk about anything degrading towards anyone. They wanted me to have a Ryan Seacrest type of radio show.

"Woah now. I'm getting high ratings for what I do. You told me I could be the DJ and run a show that made sales." I tried to plead my case, but this was CBS radio, and they had pressure from the higher ups. Now, it was all on me to comply with the new direction they were heading in. I didn't know how to handle this. I was frustrated, enraged even. How was I supposed to change? Did they want me to be boring? I didn't know how to do that. I had never been in radio because I loved the business or wanted to be a solid broadcaster; I just wanted to bring the inner side of myself out for the world to hear and make people laugh.

That night, I went on the air and kept my show exactly as inappropriate and vulgar as always. This made the bosses' decision easy. The next week I was brought into the program director's office and told that they would not be renewing my contract; that day would be my last day in the radio station.

When something like this happens in life, you would think it should be a total melt down and self-destruction, but it wasn't. I couldn't help but think of everything I went through and all the obstacles I had to overcome. I started with nothing but a dream, and I did what nobody thought was possible. To think, a kid that had everyone tell him "you couldn't do this" and "this won't ever happen", did it.

I want to tell you, I stood up and gave them the middle finger before walking out half naked with nothing but my pride, but I had seen this coming and gracefully accepted their decision. If you have ever made it from the bottom to the top in any industry, you can understand the frustration and disappointment I was going through. At the end of the day, this was just how things went. I can't say I wasn't torn up about it. Everything inside of me wanted to go across the street to the competitor and give it back to them, but that night, as I sat in front of the water show at Bellagio, I looked around at everything I had accomplished.

I set out on a vision quest in life and did everything they told me I couldn't do. I proved everyone wrong but more than that, I showed myself that if I wanted it badly enough, I could go out there and take it. Having a drink that night on the strip, I thought about everyone who had doubted me, everyone who told me this would never happen. I was a high school dropout with no formal education or training, and by the time I was nineteen years old, I had already operated three radio shows in three different states, pulling number two in the rankings in Las Vegas.

I told myself that night that I would always stay true to myself and never let someone else dictate my path in life. Leaving Las Vegas could have been very emotional experience with tears, sadness and everything that accompanies failure and broken dreams, but I was a winner. I didn't win at slot machines or at the blackjack table, but in life. I thought about all the great inspirational people that had accomplished their dreams and goals in life, and I couldn't help but smile while looking at the city that I left my mark on. I drove down the strip one last time heading back to Florida to the next adventure in my life. I knew then, listening to Frank Sinatra's "That's life" on Las Vegas Blvd, that anything I decide to do from now on, I would give my all and win.